Awaken
THE MAGIC
WITHIN

SecrETS to Living a Happy
and Fulfilled Life

TABLE OF CONTENTS

INTRODUCTION

Welcome to our collaborative book, Awaken The Magic Within: Secrets to Living a Happy and Fulfilled Life

The book is a Wisdom from the Collective: Insights and Inspiration from 10 Visionary Thinkers.

We are thrilled to present this unique collection of perspectives from 10 diverse authors who have come together to share their wisdom, knowledge, and experience.

Firstly, we would like to extend our sincerest gratitude to each of our authors who have contributed their time, energy, and expertise to create this valuable resource.

Each author brings a unique perspective and set of experiences to the table, making this book a rich tapestry of ideas and insights.

In Awaken The Magic Within, you will find a wide range of topics explored, from personal development to business strategy, spirituality to science, and everything in between.

The authors offer their best practices, insights, and wisdom to help readers navigate the complexities of modern life, find their purpose, and create a fulfilling and successful life.

Whether you're a student, entrepreneur, spiritual seeker, or simply someone looking to expand your horizons, this book has something for you.

We invite you to dive into the pages of Awaken The Magic Within 'Wisdom from the Collective' and explore the perspectives of these 10 visionary thinkers. We're confident that their collective wisdom will inspire, challenge, and empower you to achieve your own goals and dreams.

Fran Harper

Business Mentor, Master Trainer, NLP,
Timeline Therapy, Hypnosis,
#1 Best-Selling Author,
Keynote Speaker and Radio
www.tioep.com.au fran.harper.79
fran@theinstituteofempoweredpsychology.com

Fran is a successful Global Sales and Marketing Director, has established several markets for the Food and Coaching Industries. with Strong communication skills she is a resourceful, unstoppable Company Director and a Member of the Australian Institute of Company Directors. (MAICD)

She is a proven Business Mentor, helping Business Owners and Directors create work/ life balance through drawing on her 35 years of business experience.

Fran has helped many CEO's/Business owners succeed in their businesses by helping them to create and maintain clarity and Focus.

Fran is particularly versed in restructuring and helping Business Owners focus on the MMA's. (Money Making Activities)

She is a Master Trainer in NLP, Timeline Therapy & Hypnosis and a Founder of the Institute of Empowered Psychology and she has trained students from all over the world to become successful NLP TLT & Hypnosis coaches and alternative therapists.

She is a #1 Best-Selling Author "Empowered Women in Business." which launched at #1 on Amazon.

She is a Keynote Speaker and does Live Radio interviews. She will soon be featured in an upcoming TedX talk.

She is the current Winner of the Australian Channel 7 TV Show Change Labz Challenge 2022.

Her strong communication skills and natural ability has seen her Co-Found and Direct Multiple businesses, the oldest established in 1988. She has worked across numerous industries and draws experience from the Food Industry, manufacturing, insolvency, construction and Education and Training.

Fran Co-Founded The Rugby Business Network Australia and has hosted events all over the world in Rugby union and Sevens.

She is a mother of 4 successful children, a bowel cancer survivor, an avid traveler, an accomplished horsewoman and springer spaniel lover.

CHAPTER ONE

WHY HAPPINESS AND FULFILLMENT ARE SO IMPORTANT, WHY WE ALL DESERVE THEM, AND HOW TO START TO FIND THEM!

By Fran Harper

This may sound like a simple question "What makes you happy and fulfilled?"

However simple it may seem on the surface, it's a question I have found to be an extremely complex and emotional one, that I wasn't initially able to answer easily. Mainly because over the years and the treadmill of life, I hadn't stopped to really think about what made me happy ?

You may be one of the lucky ones who has been through the process of knowing exactly what makes you tick, and I applaud you; there are so many people not living in alignment, those, like me, living by the values and beliefs bestowed upon them by someone else.

Without ever really discovering your own happiness and fulfillment, not understanding that we all have the choice, choice to choose our own paths and journey. The secret is it's essential if you are to find your own truth and discover the root of your own happiness and fulfillment.

This chapter sets out to discover not only what makes you Happy and fulfilled, but also gives a few simple exercises to help you discover happiness and fulfillment if that is something that has eluded you until now. Take the time and make it a priority! Time and energy are irreplaceable, so start to use them both wisely and believe wholeheartedly that you deserve happiness and fulfillment. If you don't feel this at the moment, please use my permission as a small gift from me to you, to try to prioritize this because when you do, everything will change. Perspective, gratitude, and what you attract into your world becomes very different. Try it, and I wish you happiness and fulfillment in everything you do

When I was first asked the question, "what makes you Happy?"

I squirmed in my seat, deafened by the silence, noticeably overwhelmed with sadness.

I felt awkward and physically uncomfortable; Kim, my first-ever Life coach, remained quiet, acknowledging me only with a slight nod, saying nothing, maintaining a sacred space.

He had been asking me the same question for around four weeks; I wasn't able to answer him with any clarity; each time, he held the space and let me reflect and try to articulate what I was searching for, always being reduced to tears and feelings of overwhelming sadness. Sharing only what I didn't want and what made me unhappy.

I was a mother of 5 and a successful businesswoman, but I wasn't happy in my relationship; the lack of quality communication had eroded the connection with my Husband, I was lonely and miserable.

Working long hours in the family business, ferrying kids to all the sporting events that were on, and of course, the 4.30 am starts for swimming training and rowing, etc., etc.

I know that for many people, this can be the norm, and the word that had me totally stuck was DUTY – it was my duty to do all of the things.

It was my choice, and I often wonder now what was driving the necessity, but that's a whole other chapter.

It happened, and I forgot myself. I forgot the importance of making sure I was OK. I forgot to look after myself. The conflict is eating away at me and keeping me busier and busier to numb the void in my heart.

I was on autopilot, a chameleon, the high achieving and successful Businesswomen, mother of successful children, whilst all the time empty and dissatisfied, adhered to by the total indifference of my partner who wasn't emotionally or physically there to support me.

The love we once shared was replaced with silence and separate rooms and eventually divorce.

Ironically within three weeks of leaving the Marriage, I was diagnosed with Stage 3 Bowel Cancer and underwent major surgery & Chemo; if nothing else, severe illness can focus the mind on what's truly important and give you the ability to really focus on the things that matter.

It was Kim, my Life Coach, who first made me aware that Happiness and fulfillment are major components to my overall well-being and that I needed to be able to find my own happiness.

It wasn't anyone else's responsibility to make me happy.

In fact, I could not tell anyone what made me happy or what I needed to be fulfilled because I just didn't know!

My life was a series of plays, each with a different persona and each playing out as a charade of what was expected of me – the self-imposed duties I had placed on myself that left me no time for self-care and for finding my own happy place.

I can't change the years that I felt sad, lonely, or conflicted by staying in a situation that had run its course, but I can share my experience, and if that gives a small insight and inspiration to change aspects of life that aren't working for you right now if it allows anyone to make their time and energy precious than I am pleased to share.

There is no decision worth making that keeps you unfulfilled and unhappy.

This chapter sets out to discover not only what makes you Happy and fulfilled but also a few simple exercises to help you discover happiness and fulfillment if that is something that has eluded you until now. Take the time and make it a priority!

Time and energy are irreplaceable, so start to use them both wisely, believe wholeheartedly that you deserve happiness and fulfillment.

If you don't feel this at the moment, please use my permission as a small gift from me to you to prioritize you because when you do, everything you do will change. When you're run ragged, it's up to you to add the boundaries and look after yourself too.

There is only so long you can neglect yourself and your own happiness before the universe brings you consequences. So, if you want to be in charge of your own life, happiness, and fulfillment, then start today. No one can do this for you, and it's imperative to your environment and microsystem that you spend time focusing on it. No one else can make you happy or fulfilled; that's all up to you.

When you take personal responsibility for your own happiness and fulfillment, your perspective, gratitude, and what you attract into your world becomes very different. Try it, and I wish you happiness and fulfillment in everything you do; that's not being one of those crazy over the top positive people but having an inner contentment that creates its own magnetic attraction.

So, if you're tired of feeling like a grumpy gringeon, as my kids used to call me, tired of feeling unfulfilled and unhappy in your personal and professional life, then don't think you're alone; you most definitely are not! Unfortunately, this is a very common state of mind, and as perception is projection, all too often, poor communication will result in most things you take on.

So, think about that, reflect, and make a list of situations where communication was affected adversely when you were feeling unhappy or unfulfilled?

Don't worry; there's hope for even the grimmest of grim reapers. You can change things!

Let's start with the personal side of things.

When you're feeling unhappy and unfulfilled, it's like trying to put on your socks with oven mitts on; everything is just a little bit harder.

You may find yourself slouching on the couch watching reruns of "Keeping Up with the Kardashians" instead of going for that hike you've been promising yourself for weeks.

Or maybe you're reaching for that pint of ice cream in the fridge instead of the veggies in the crisper. And let's not even get started on your love life or lack thereof. Everything is at odds.

Now let's move on to the professional side of things. When you're feeling down and out, it's like trying to close a sale with a broken arm or trying to light a fire with a damp matchstick.

You may find yourself procrastinating, avoiding calls and emails, and generally just not giving it your all. Your productivity takes a nosedive, and your clients start to notice; let's not forget about your colleagues; they may start to think you're grumpy, always raining on their parade.

But, just like a broken arm can be fixed, and a damp matchstick can be dried, there is hope for even the grimmest of grim reapers. By taking the time to identify what brings you happiness and fulfillment, you can start to make small changes in your life that can make a big difference. Maybe it's taking a yoga class, picking up a new hobby, or just spending more time with the people you love. Whatever it is, it's important to remember that happiness and fulfillment are not destinations; they're journeys.

And when it comes to the professional side of things, it's important to remember that happiness and fulfillment don't just make us better employees; they make us better business owners too. When we're feeling good, we're more likely to be productive, creative and to make better decisions.

In addition to the improved productivity and decision-making, being happy and fulfilled as a business owner also has other benefits.

For one, a positive attitude and outlook can have a contagious effect on employees, leading to a more positive and productive work environment. Happy and fulfilled business owners are also more likely to foster strong relationships with customers, suppliers, and other business partners, which can lead to better opportunities and more successful deals.

Furthermore, when a business owner is fulfilled and happy, they can also set a positive example for their employees, encouraging them to also prioritize their own well-being and happiness, which can lead to a more engaged and motivated workforce.

Additionally, happy and fulfilled business owners tend to have a more holistic approach to business; they understand that it's not all about making money or growing their business; it's also about their own personal growth and development.

They care about the impact of their business on the environment and the community and work towards creating a positive impact, which can lead to a better reputation and branding for their business. In short, being happy and fulfilled is not just a nice-to-have for business owners; it's a necessity.

When business owners prioritize their well-being, they are more likely to make better decisions, foster strong relationships, create a positive work environment, set a positive example, and create a positive impact, which ultimately leads to a more successful and sustainable business.

Working with a business coach can be an important step for business owners in achieving happiness and fulfillment. A coach can provide valuable support and guidance as business owners navigate the challenges of entrepreneurship and strive to achieve their personal and professional goals.

One of the main benefits of working with a coach is that they can help business owners to gain clarity and focus on what they truly want to achieve. A coach can help business owners to set meaningful and attainable goals and then create a plan to achieve them. They can provide valuable insights and feedback to help business owners to overcome obstacles and stay on track towards their goals.

Additionally, coaches can also help business owners to develop a sense of balance and perspective. They can help to identify areas of the business owner's life that may be out of balance and provide strategies and tools to help them regain equilibrium. This can be particularly important for business owners, who often find it challenging to balance the demands of running a business with their personal lives.

Moreover, business coaches can also provide a sounding board and a source of accountability. They can help business owners to stay motivated and focused and provide encouragement and support when things get tough. They are also able to provide the business owners with a different perspective and an unbiased opinion, which can be valuable for solving problems and making important decisions.

Furthermore, coaches can also help business owners to improve their communication and relationships. They can provide guidance on how to effectively communicate with employees, customers, and other stakeholders, which can lead to more positive and productive relationships.

In conclusion, working with a business coach can be an important step for business owners in achieving happiness and fulfillment. They can help business owners to gain clarity, set meaningful goals, develop a sense of balance, provide accountability, and improve relationships. By working with a coach, business owners can gain the tools and support they need to create a successful and fulfilling business, which can ultimately lead to a happier and more satisfying personal life.

So why don't people know what makes them happy?

There are many reasons why people may not know what makes them happy. Some of the most common reasons include;

- ***Societal pressure:***

Society often dictates what we should find happiness and fulfillment in, such as financial success, material possessions, and status.

As a result, many people may feel unsure of what truly brings them happiness and fulfillment.

- ***Lack of self-awareness***:

Many people may not have taken the time to reflect on their own needs, values, and desires, making it difficult to identify what brings them happiness and fulfillment.

Fear of change: Knowing what makes us happy may also require us to make changes to our lives, such as leaving a job, ending a relationship, or moving to a new location.

For some people, the idea of change can be daunting and prevent them from identifying what makes them happy.

- *Past Experiences:*

People who have experienced a lot of trauma or negative experiences may have learned to suppress or ignore their desires and emotions. These people may have a harder time identifying what brings them happiness and fulfillment.

- *External validation:*

Some people might find their happiness and fulfillment through external validation or external factors such as the opinion of others, the number of likes on social media. They may forget the importance of self-validation and don't focus on what truly makes them happy.

- *Unawareness of the importance of self-care:*

Many people may not realize the importance of self-care in finding happiness and fulfillment. Without taking care of oneself, it may be difficult to identify what brings joy and fulfillment to life.

By recognizing these barriers, people can take steps to overcome them, such as setting aside time for self-reflection, seeking guidance and support, and being open to change. With the right mindset and approach, anyone can discover what makes them happy and fulfilled.

Here's a usef ul exercise to help with Self Reflection and identifying what makes you happy start A Gratitude journal

Here's how to do it, and I recommend to everyone to do this, even if it's once a week! The benefits are exponential, everyone has heard of this, but it requires discipline to become effective at your gratitude journal.

1. Buy a nice notebook – (I would also like to buy a nice pen!)
2. Set aside time: Choose a time of day when you can sit down and focus on your thoughts and feelings. It can be in the morning, evening, or anytime you prefer.
3. Reflect: Take a few moments to think about the things that bring you happiness and fulfillment. These can be big or small things, things that happen regularly, or things you would like to happen more often.
4. Write it down: Once you have a list of things that make you happy, write them down in your journal.
5. Reflect some more: Take some time to think about why these things make you happy. What is it about them that brings you joy and fulfillment?
6. Repeat: repeat the process of self-reflection and writing things down in the journal at least once a week or more regularly if desired.
7. Review: After some weeks or a month, you can look back at your journal and review the things that made you happy and fulfilled. This will give you an idea of what you want to prioritize in your life, and make sure to make time for those things.

This exercise helps you to focus on the things that bring you joy and fulfillment, and it also helps you to be more aware of the positive things in your life. By writing them down, you have a visual representation of what brings you happiness, and you can refer to it whenever you need a reminder of the things you want to prioritize in your life.

Additionally, reflecting on the reasons why these things make you happy can give you a deeper understanding of yourself, and this can help you to make more informed decisions about your life.

Living a happy and fulfilled life is something that many people strive for, but it can be difficult to know where to begin.

There are countless books, articles, and self-help gurus that offer their own unique advice on how to live a happy and fulfilled life, but it can be hard to know what to believe and where to start.

Here I am exploring some of the key concepts and strategies for living a happy and fulfilled life and why it is so important.

First, it is important to recognize that happiness is not a destination or a permanent state of being. Rather, it is a journey, and like any journey, there will be ups and downs. The key is to learn how to navigate the lows and appreciate the highs. One way to do this is to focus on the present moment. We often get caught up in regrets about the past or worries about the future, but the only moment we can truly experience is the present.

By focusing on the present, we can learn to appreciate the simple things in life and be grateful for what we have.

Another important aspect of living a happy and fulfilled life is to have a sense of purpose. When we have a sense of purpose, we are more likely to feel motivated and engaged in our lives. This can come from a career, a passion, or a cause that we care about. It is important to find something that aligns with our values and gives you a sense of meaning and purpose. A way to find a sense of purpose can be making a list of what we are passionate about and aligning that with the goals we want to achieve in life.

In addition to having a sense of purpose, it is also important to build strong, supportive relationships with friends and loved ones. Having a strong social support system can help us cope with stress and provide a sense of belonging and connection. It also can be important to have healthy boundaries, knowing when to say no to things that don't align with our values and goals.

Self-care is also an important aspect of living a happy and fulfilled life. This can include things like getting enough sleep, eating a healthy diet, exercising regularly, and taking time for activities that we enjoy. It's important to focus on the physical, emotional, and mental aspect of self-care, taking time for self-reflection and practicing mindfulness.

It's important to remember that happiness and fulfillment are not dependent on any external circumstances. We often think that if we just had more money, a better job, or a different partner, we would be happy. But the truth is, true happiness and fulfillment come from within. It is not something that can be bought or acquired; it must be cultivated.

By focusing on the present, finding a sense of purpose, building strong relationships, practicing self-care, and cultivating a positive mindset, we can take the first steps towards living a happy and fulfilled life.

Living a happy and fulfilled life is an ongoing process that requires effort and commitment. It's important to remember that there's no one-size-fits-all solution; what works for one person may not work for another. But by focusing on the present moment, finding a sense of purpose, building strong relationships, practicing self-care, and cultivating a positive mindset, we can take the first steps towards living a happy and fulfilled life. It is important as it affects not only our own well-being but also those around us and the impact we make in the world. Taking the time and effort to live a happy and fulfilled life is worth it.

When we fully appreciate and recognize that happiness is a state of mind. We all have moments of joy, contentment, and satisfaction, but we also experience sadness, disappointment, and pain. It is a natural part of being human. The key is to learn how to manage our thoughts and emotions, so we can focus on the positive aspects of our lives.

One way to do this is to practice mindfulness, which helps us to be present at the moment and to focus on the things that matter most. When we are present at the moment, we can appreciate the simple things in life, like the warmth of the sun on our skin or the sound of birds singing. These small moments of joy and contentment can add up over time and bring us a sense of overall well-being.

Another crucial aspect of living a happy and fulfilled life is to have a sense of purpose. When we have a sense of purpose, we are more likely to feel motivated and engaged in our lives. This can come from a career, a passion, or a cause that we care about. It is important to find something that aligns with our values and gives us a sense of meaning and purpose.

A way to find a sense of purpose is by looking at our passions and aligning that with the goals we want to achieve in life.

Whether it's writing a book, volunteering, or starting a business, having something to work towards and something that we are passionate about can bring great fulfillment and satisfaction in life.

But, as important as having a sense of purpose is, it's also vital to have strong, supportive relationships with friends and loved ones. It's essential to surround ourselves with people who understand us and support us. Having a strong social support system can help us cope with stress and provide a sense of belonging and connection. It also can be important to have healthy boundaries, knowing when to say no to things that don't align with our values and goals. It's not always easy to build strong relationships, but it's worth the effort. The love and support of the people we care about can be a source of strength, and it can help us through the tough times.

Self-care is also an essential aspect of living a happy and fulfilled life. This can include things like getting enough sleep, eating a healthy diet, exercising regularly, and taking time for activities that we enjoy. It's important to focus on the physical, emotional, and mental aspect of self-care, taking time for self-reflection and practicing mindfulness.

We can't pour from an empty cup; taking care of ourselves is the first step to being able to take care of others.

However, you are living your life now, a good indicator that you are not as happy and fulfilled as you could be; maybe you are still blaming others for the outcomes you are experiencing; look at this long and hard and start to be aware of where you add blame for your feelings outside of yourself.

Ultimately you can change how you react to certain situations; it may not be easy, but being aware will start the process.

Taking responsibility and putting in those boundaries for yourself, knowing what you need and what makes you happy, allows you to refocus your energies on this and start to create a happy and fulfilled life.

The consequences of not being true to yourself and not allowing the time for self-reflection can be traumatic and will allow the cycle of unhappiness to continue; I know because I did it for over 20 years; what was I thinking?

In truth, I wasn't thinking about me; I was thinking about the kids, business, cash flow, everything that had to be done, and not taking time for me.

If my experience sheds a little light on the possibility of change and finding happiness and fulfillment, then I am happy to share.

I am single now, and I have 4 amazing children; sadly, my stepdaughter blames me; I hope that she, too, will find happiness and fulfillment one day when she finds her own happiness. Until that day, I will be here for her; however, I now know from experience that no good will come from setting expectations of others, as that leads to disappointment; we cannot control the actions or thoughts of others.

We can only work from our own heart space and stay on a committed journey to finding our own happiness and fulfillment, which will, in turn, bring our true tribe along with us in harmony and love.

My journey of self-awareness started with NLP and a Practitioner course, which took me through NLP, hypnosis, and Timeline therapy, a lot of self-reflection, and a lot of tissues!

I went on to train as a Master Trainer in NLP, Time Line Therapy, and Hypnosis and now train several courses per year at all levels.

I integrate my Business Mentoring with Mindfulness and training other Coaches to train as Trainers and to succeed in their businesses while maintaining or creating a sense of self.

I am a #1 best-selling Author, "Empowered Women in Business," Keynote Speaker, Host of the NLP Global Summit, Master Trainer, Multiple Business Owner, the oldest established in 1988.

Selena DORSEY

Global Events Producer & #1 International Best-Selling Author

Website: Selenad.com

Instagram: @selenadofficial

Selena D. is a global events producer, producing over a dozen profitable summits in less than two years including, Law of Attraction Word Summit,

Empowered Women In Business Summit, Podcast Expert Summit, Faster EFT Summit, and many others.

She is the #1 International Best-Selling Author and Publisher of "Empowered Women In Business", which went #1 on Amazon in 24 hours in 6 categories, including, Business Teams (Australia), Retirement Planning, Business Mentorship & Coaching and Women's Spirituality & Spiritual healing.

Selena lives with her family in the New York Metro Area.

CHAPTER TWO

5 STEPS TO MANIFESTING ANYTHING YOU WANT

By Selena Dorsey

Take a moment to think about everything you want to be, do, or have. Dream big because you've got the energy flying and surging through you right now that you can direct it for what you want.

In 2006, I was introduced to the Law of Attraction by sheer coincidence. And at that point, not many people knew about it. While it's been in discussion since the 1800's, it wasn't until the movie *The Secret* that more people became familiar with this inner power they could use to their advantage. Everyone had already been using it in their lives, but unconsciously, they were blind to it. And I was too. It took an early book, Michael Losier's Law of Attraction, to help me understand what the Law of Attraction was and how to get a handle on it.

A year later, I experienced tragedy, as close relatives passed away, leading me into a dark and depressed place. I knew I had to take matters into my own hands and get myself back into a more positive mental space, so I started seeking out mindset coaches. My goal was to find joy and redirect my thoughts and energy.

This perhaps began my discovery and love of self-help books. They really can help so many people that are going through tough times and recalibrate. I always advise anyone going through a difficult time to pick up a book - it has the power to change your life. To date, I've read hundreds of personal development books because I'm still learning. And through my learning, I've come up with five quick thoughts that may jump start your process.

- The very first thought is to know and understand what you ***don't*** want. And that's useful because most people are stuck there and need help figuring out where to go. Oftentimes, we're clear on what we want in our lives, but are unable to remove the things that may be holding us back. These can be things we ***don't*** want that still linger for a number of reasons, including a lack of self-awareness or even subconscious blind spots. It's by recognizing these things that can help us gain clarity and focus on what we are seeking.
- Second, you must change your complaint into an intention. Intentions are so crucial because they are effectively objectives. They are statements of what you want to have, do, or be. But a lot of people don't know how to state one. So when you look at the first step, your "complaint", and you might say, "I don't like not having money in my pocket", or "I'm tired of being broke". Instead of that complaint, the intention would be, I want more than enough money to pay my bills, or I intend to be independently wealthy. Or if the first complaint was, "I'm tired of being alone", the intention would now be to attract my soulmate, or my life partner.
- Next, we refer to the common occurrence that whenever we decide to do something, we state our intention, and may have negativity bubble up. It's a negativity or limiting belief in our subconscious

mind, unconscious mind, and conscious mind. And unless we clear those beliefs, they can stop, stall, or slow us down. So very simply, clearing those limiting beliefs in effect clears the way to move forward. It's ultimately incumbent on you to be honest about what they are.

- The fourth step is an advanced visualization technique. Most people are told to visualize what they want to have. If you want to have more money, you visualize more capital. You want to have your soulmate, you visualize being with somebody. But you must assume you *already* have your intention so that you can feel what it's like to live it, to have it - and embody it now so you think it's real. The whole purpose of feeling it's real is that it will accelerate the attraction to it.

- Lastly, it's essential to let go while taking inspired action. And that confuses a lot of people. To let go means to let go of your attachment to things being a certain way. You're not limiting the possibilities by saying, "it has to be this person", or "it has to be this much money", or "it has to come from this direction". You're allowing the universe to naturally align with your goal - or something even better.

Always remember that you are a gift. You're making a difference in someone's life, your life, and everyone you touch. Keep that in mind as you navigate your own journey and continue to grow.

Dr. Olga Zabora, PsyD

**International Best Selling Author/ Speaker/
Certified Master NLP Coach/ NLP Trainer's Trainer**

http://goddessevent.com/

https://drolgazabora.com/

Dr. Olga Zabora, PsyD, CHT, Holds a Doctorate Degree in Clinical Psychology from the US, a Diploma of Clinical Hypnotherapy from HMI, and multiple certifications, including Gestalt Therapy at PGI and Jungian Analytical Psychology at Jung Institute of Los Angeles, Past Life Regression & Spiritual Regression with Dr. Brian Weiss, MD and trained with Dr. Richard Bandler, co-founder of Neuro-Linguistic Programming.

She was a collaborating author in a book called: Transform Your Wounds into Wisdom is the #1 Amazon International Best Seller 2022 and also collaborated on a second project, Master Your Mindset, published in February 2023 and became an international bestseller on Amazon as well. She is getting her book published in 2023.

Dr. Olga's extensive training in the US and outside the country, combined with 20 years of education and experience, allows for forward-thinking, advanced knowledge, and flexibility. In addition, her love for life and people will enable you to create transformational changes.

Her far-reaching personal experiences and deep exploration of Jungian Therapy, Dream Analysis, Holotropic Breathwork® with Dr. Stan Grof, meditation, mindfulness, yoga, Philosophical Tantra, Sacred Temple Mandala Dance in India, Multiple studies about Feminine Nature and Energy from world-renowned professionals.

Dr. Olga holds Certificate from Optimum Health Institute and Advanced Nutritional and Integrative Medicine for Mental Health Professionals. Shamanic Studies from Michael Harner's Foundation and other spiritual practices has allowed her to integrate her knowledge and utilize it in assisting clients with their life journeys and lasting positive changes.

Her passion lies in helping you become aware of your resources by bringing up the best parts of yourself to guide you gently with your conscious transformation into the best and happiest version of yourself.

Dr. Olga continues publishing her books, clinical practice, coaching, teaching classes, and conducting empowering women's retreats. In addition, she shares her humor, knowledge, and experience with everyone attending her courses at www.GoddessEvent.com & DrOlgaZabora.com, IG: @ unleashingthegoddess

---

CHAPTER THREE

HOW TO FIND, REFINE & REDEFINE YOURSELF IN THE MIDST OF THE STORM OF YOUR LIFE USING 5 SIMPLE TECHNIQUES

by Dr. Olga Zabora, PsyD, CHT.

Disclaimer: Any techniques listed and explained here do not substitute mental health therapy or advice. If any methods feel overwhelming, please find the right therapist, coach, or hypnotherapist to help you.

M agic… What is magic? How many of us experienced it, especially in childhood?

Is it something unexplainable, and yet we feel this, and we are in an "awe" state when we see it, isn't it? Everybody wants to have magic in one way or another in our lives, don't we?

Magic looks effortless. A good example is when we watch a movie where the character is facing a challenge or is in a disempowered state, and one, two, three with a snap of the fingers: and at the end of the movie, we see him transformed. He is reaping the rewards of life: getting the most beautiful girl, money, wealth, recognition, or success. That is all portrayed in Hollywood movies, right? In fairy tales and mythology, we see the heroic journey as well. A hero wins the battles, acquires unique qualities, or uses "magical tools," like Harry Potter.

What if you will discover this secret of a few "magical tools" so you can awaken the magic within yourself?

What if you acquire a magical roadmap that will take you to the desired results faster and with less energy expended? What if I share some techniques to help you find your way through hardships or challenges and ignite the magic within?

What if you will be amazed by how quickly you can change your emotional state or state of mind and become a success like many others who can control their mind and manage their emotions? What if you knew how to refine and redefine yourself through the challenges you go through and become the best version of yourself and no longer be defined by your past?

Based on my experience with so much work done on myself and working with clients, I teach many techniques that create excellent transformative results in my client's lives, which I'm happy to share in this chapter.

Most likely, you have all heard about conscious and subconscious minds, approximately 10% vs 90%. In other words, the conscious mind is the goal-setter, and the subconscious mind is the goal-getter with 90% of the subconscious resources. In Neuro-Linguistic Programming, one of the presuppositions of NLP is that all learning happens on subconscious level: beyond conscious awareness.

Dr. Milton H. Erickson, psychiatrist and hypnotherapist, was creating excellent results and positive changes in his clients, seemingly effortlessly and magically. How? Through metaphors that bypass the critical conscious mind. He was very successful at that. Dr. Richard Bandler and Dr. John Grinder, the founders of Neuro-Linguistic Programming, studied his work style and discovered the language patterns that work well on a subconscious level. They had Dr. Milton H. Erickson's methods as part of the NLP system: his communication style directly to the subconscious mind rather than the conscious through stories and symbols like we encounter in our dreams or in fairy tales as well that is called: Milton Model.

Since the early tribal times, humans have learned through storytelling when wisdom has passed from generation to generation. It's ingrained in us. We are so mesmerized by movies, fairy tales, and myths portraying the heroic journey, don't we? We all like to watch the transformation and victory over challenges. You too can be the hero of your daily life by controlling the thoughts of your mind and celebrating your accomplishments of magical transformation.

So, one way to create magic is through communication with your subconscious mind: talk to yourself lovingly and respectfully and your relationship with your body will start changing, as well as your relationships with people and life in general. Another magical tool is the visualization technique that you may use. It is also connected to your subconscious mind because you use images that are the symbolic language of your subconscious mind. Magic happens, especially when you utilize the body-mind connection by creating congruence between the conscious and subconscious minds. This can be done through hypnosis or self-hypnosis that you may learn. It's exciting, isn't it?

Have you ever paid attention to how magic shows up in your life? Have you ever experienced synchronicities or instant manifestation: the right person shows up, or resources and opportunities appear from nowhere, and miraculous healing happens? I'm sure you want to know more about your powerful mind, don't you?

Let's look at the components of magic from a psychological point of view and how to awaken the magic within.

Based on my experience with my clients, I see that one of the main ingredients is a right mindset or "elevated mindset," as I called it in the previous work in collaboration with John Spender's series of books: A Journey of Riches, called Master Your Mindset in Chapter "The Breakthrough with an Elevated Mindset," just recently published in February 2023 and became an international bestseller on Amazon.

Also, as we see in a movie or in a mythological story or a fairy tale of transformation it always requires courage from a hero. Another magical transformational component is a guide who will help you on your journey or at least having a map and knowledge about the power of your mind, human behavior, and psychology will lay out the plan for you. And last but not least is to practice your new choices, behavior, and thought process long enough until it becomes your new habitual self, your new homeostasis.

Since we are not immune from life, we all go through challenges and difficulties at some point in our lives. We all experience life transitions, changing homes, losing a job, getting a new job, having a period of adjustment, divorce, empty nests, grief, etc. Not to forget that we just went through a global pandemic, lockdowns, isolation, and losses. This "magical map" will serve you as a basic guide to create changes in your mindset and you can use this guide by yourself. So you can make magic within even if you go through challenges: the storms in our lives.

In the first part, I'll share with you the simple yet powerful techniques you can use to self-regulate your emotional and mental states. I use these techniques all the time with my clients and myself. These techniques will allow you to find yourself, your unique heartbeat, and your unique breath pattern. Learning the basics first: connecting to your body, your physical essence. I'll share the exercises on regulating your body, such as breathing and listening to your heartbeat. As Dr. Jack Kornfield said: "Attention to the human body brings healing and regeneration. Through awareness of the body we remember who we really are."

In the second part, you will learn some techniques that will help you to elevate your mindset and refine your thought process, then learn how to become a more refined version of yourself.

The third part will teach you how to live your powerful self, continue making different choices, see new opportunities, and redefine yourself.

If you are ready to dive in, let's begin…

PART ONE: FIND YOURSELF

I've heard very often from so many clients that they feel lost… no direction, or not knowing what decision to make. So let's learn how you can "find yourself" when you feel lost or overwhelmed emotionally, in other words: in the midst of the storm of your life that all of us are going through one way or another, like transiting through challenging periods of life. What works well is to find the pulse on your wrist or place your palm on your heart and pause... Just listen... Connect with yourself through the heartbeat... Stay still and listen... Listen to your heartbeat...

Did you know that no other person has the same heartbeat or cardiogram as you? It is unique for you, only you! As Dr. Milton H. Erickson said: "You are as unique as your fingerprint." Thus recognize yourself as a unique expression of life, an exceptional human being. No one as you existed before, and no one would be like you after. Once you connect with yourself through the heartbeat and recognize your uniqueness - this is one of the expressions of self-love and self-value. Practice this exercise for a few minutes daily, then journal what has changed. What magic appears in your life? What awareness surfaced up from this observation? You may journal about this.

Calm awareness creates stillness in your mind when you are aware of the beat of your heart and focus on this process. This fundamental self-regulation takes us to the first experience of feeling the mother's heartbeat in her womb. Connecting with our own heartbeat brings us to that calm, safe, and secure state. Next step is to start paying attention to your breath. If it's shallow and short, then consciously start deepening it and elongating it. Stop, listen, and feel your breath as the ocean's waves: breathe in and out. Cherish yourself, give yourself self-love: breathe in love for yourself, breathe out love for others... Breathe in and out... Feel the constant movement of life force moving through you, constantly creating you, observing this creation process in stillness. Jot down a few words about this experience.

Have you ever noticed that thoughts and breath are interrelated? The faster the thoughts are racing through your mind, the faster and more shallow your breath becomes. Conversely, breathing deeper and slower has a calming effect on the nervous system. In addition, you may "clear" your head from the thoughts and practice observing them as clouds in a clear blue sky, just watching them and not being attached to any of them. Creating this "detachment" helps you to observe your life's challenges from a higher perspective, increasing the wisdom and the way you look at your

difficulties. Also, remember that there is always a rainbow after the storm, and the sun always shines behind the clouds. It's up to you to change your perspective or not. It is your choice, and it's in your power.

By doing so, you create space in your mind and life itself for something you want to focus on, manifest on your life journey. Remember, whatever you focus on - the more it shows up in your life. Have you ever experienced that?

Techniques:

1. Observe your breath and your heartbeat.
2. Connect to your body, and recognize your uniqueness.
3. Give yourself self-love: breath in love for yourself, breathe out love for others.

PART TWO: REFINE YOURSELF

After practicing the first steps to create magic, you learned how to "find yourself" through the breath and your heartbeat by connecting to your body. Here is the second part, you can now know how to "refine yourself" by refining your thought process, being very selective and focused using the power of your mind, so the life challenges no longer define you but refine you.

There are many powerful techniques here you can utilize to awaken the magic in your mind: self-hypnosis or using affirmation cards and placing them on your mirror or fridge, or by hanging your vision board next to your bed, so you can see it the first thing when you wake up and the last thing you see before you go to sleep.

You can also practice mindful walking or mindful eating that will increase your awareness and create the magic of savoring every moment in your life, especially when you're eating mindfully: eating very slowly, as slow as you can, amplifying your tastebuds and enjoying many "colors" of flavors as simple as eating your favorite piece of fruit. Try this "magic," and you will be amazed at how much we may miss every day if we do not engage all of our senses but overload ourselves with only visual information that is always readily available and streams from everywhere. So take good care of yourself, and be intentional in what you want to create.

As a part of the process of refining your mind, I would like to share another effective technique, such as the journaling exercise, that can help to release negative emotions and discharge energy. Writing with your hand has more effect as if you are typing. When you do your handwriting, you are connected to your body. By writing out the emotionally charged state, you externalize the problem, and you can look at it more detachedly, understanding that you can change it so it no longer defines you.

You may write the letter to someone you have a challenging relationship with but do NOT send it to them; destroy the letters in the best way at your discrepancy. The healing power of writing a letter that I shared in the chapter in the series A Journey of Riches international bestseller book on Amazon called - "Transform Your Wounds into Wisdom" in Chapter One: Heal Your Family Wounds that was published in October 2022.

A word of caution: make sure you have a safe space and be very gentle with yourself by scheduling a particular time with this process of writing a letter, so you do not have to rush to work, have enough time "close" this sacred place and process, so you can feel the boundaries and closure and to be able to perform your regular activities in life after the process is done. It is also important to schedule time to contemplate the changes, witness your insights after emptying your buffer through writing. So you have enough time to integrate changes and insights into your life.

Once you created the space for something you want, fill this space with a list of gratitude: what you are grateful for today. You can start even with One or two or three things and slowly build it up to ten. A gratitude list helps shift your focus from what you do not have to list what you have and are grateful for. So many people practiced it, including me, and it works charmingly well. Just ensure you do it consistently, and you will get the results you are looking for.

The next one is the "reframing" technique that is widely used in Neuro-Linguistic Programming and is also used in Breakthrough Sessions. If you would like to dive deeper into this, you can find more information in the book Master Your Mindset in Series: A Journey of Riches in the chapter "The Breakthrough with an Elevated Mindset."

So, what is reframing?

I often hear that when people verbalize something they would like in their lives, they use a negative sentence structure. So they use a strategy called the Neuro-Linguistic Programming "away" strategy," which gives inconsistent results. Because a person is trying to avoid something that brings him an uncomfortable or painful state, for example, poverty: "I do not want to be poor," or health: "I do not want to be sick." Instead, we redirect the mind toward what a person wants: "I want to be rich," "I want to be healthy." This strategy is the strategy called "toward" the goal rather than away.

You can also reframe the situation by moving focus to different times or settings: for example, when a parent is not happy that the child is constantly negotiating with them. How would you reframe it? This skill of negotiation will serve her to become a successful mediator attorney. So the focus of your mind now has more than one perspective on the "problem," then the flexibility of thinking brings a different state of mind, and thus you can make other choices in life, can you not?

Here is another great example that Dr. Tad James, Ph.D., Master NLP Trainer, was sharing during his training about two different points of view on the same action. One client says: "My mother never loved me…." "Why?" "Because she always folded the cloth for me in the morning, and I never had a chance to choose what to wear." The other person says: "I felt that my mother never loved me because she never folded clothes for me..." Isn't that surprising?

Or here is another example where my client was irritated that her husband would always call her to ask what kind of pizza toppings she wanted for her and her kids, even though they had been married for a decade. When she reframed the behavior of her husband and shifted from an opposing point of view: "He never remembers what I like," to the resourceful state of mind: that he wanted to please her by making sure she gets exactly what she wanted in case she wanted something new. That the same behavior was interpreted as an act of care and love rather than neglect or ignorance. The moment she was able to shift her perspective, the dynamic in her relationship changed for the better. Isn't this interesting?

Practice reframing techniques and have fun! Enjoy the magic of changing the state by reframing your point of view on the problem.

Techniques:

1. Practice mindful walking, mindful eating, and conscious action-taking.
2. Use tools like journaling, writing letters, and gratitude lists.
3. Master your mindset with the reframing technique.

PART THREE: REDEFINE YOURSELF AND LIVE YOUR POWER

Now you have experienced and practiced the magic of connecting with your body and finding yourself through these practices of observing your breath and heartbeat and giving yourself self-love and respect. You also have learned how to refine yourself through the power of your mind by using the reframing technique, journaling, gratitude list, mindful eating, and mindful walking.

In this part, let's learn how to redefine yourself through new behavior choices, thoughts, and living your new you! You already awaken the magic within yourself. Now it's time to live your magic. You would ask: how will I be able to do this?

You can do it by taking an action that may be called: "dancing in the rain." Remember you do not have to wait until the rain is going to pass. Instead, you can start dancing in the rain, knowing it's in your power to take actions with an elevated mindset.

Redefine yourself by making new choices, thinking new thoughts, evaluating your beliefs, by being congruent and persistent in your behavior and thought process. Please be patient with yourself, and yes, magic will happen. Everytime you choose a new you, you are choosing a refined and redefined new version of yourself. Be the light for others. Blaze your trail. Share your wisdom and learnings with others.

By choosing something new, we fire new neurons and wire them by practicing new behavior models and unique thought processes. We literally recreate a new person who thinks like a success and acts like a successful person. Whatever was unattainable or seemed like magic before, now is our new daily routine and new homeostasis. Learn something new and practice daily to live your bigger self, making new choices and thought processes.

One of my favorite techniques in Neuro-Linguistic Programming is "The Ring of Power," which involves the concept of anchoring. I usually teach it live. We choose six powerful states and anchor them into the imaginary ring in front of you. When I observe participants during this exercise, I see how their faces and body are beaming with the energizing wave of the renewed life force energy, which runs through them like electricity. Practitioners are experiencing this transformation, feeling so powerful and resourceful. It's like watching a change that takes place in the hero's body in one of those Hollywood movies. Participants of this training are "anchoring" the powerful state into every cell, into the whole being. Shining the light, beaming nothing but strength, confidence, and power. For more information, you may find the feedback from students who went through training and got results from "The Ring of Power" on my Youtube channel: Dr. Olga Zabora, PsyD, under the title: "What People say about "The Ring of Power."

Techniques:

1. Make new choices and choose new thoughts.
2. Create healthier rituals.
3. Practice the resourceful states by using "The Ring of Power" technique.

Obviously, you have found more than five techniques described in this chapter, but the magic is in you. You can awaken the magic within you by choosing the five techniques that resonate with you the most and practicing them for some time. So take the best, and bless the rest! Some people practice them for a week or two or even eight weeks or longer. Studies show that eight weeks of practicing rewires the brain and its structure. Dr. Joe Dispenza publishes the results of brain research in his books. So practice enough time to create the changes that you are looking for.

Most success I observed in people's lives when all five ingredients were used and practiced: connecting to your body, refining your thought process, and taking actions by making new choices and living them. Choose five techniques that resonate the most with you and awaken the magic within.

LET'S REVIEW THE TECHNIQUES:

1. Observe your breath and your heartbeat. Connect to your body, and recognize your uniqueness. Give yourself self-love: breath in love for yourself, breathe out love for others.
2. Practice mindful walking, mindful eating, and conscious action-taking.
3. Use tools like journaling, writing letters, and gratitude lists.
4. Master your mindset with the reframing technique.

5. Make new choices and choose new thoughts. Create new healthier rituals. Practice the resourceful states by using "The Ring of Power" technique.

I believe true transformation is possible when genuine desire, commitment, and courage are present! Wishing you to ignite the power of your mind and awaken the magic within so you can live a happy and fulfilled life!

Dr. Olga Zabora, PsyD

Deborah Lawrence

Certified Health & Life Coach/ Certified Trainer of the Creative Insight Journey (CIJ)

www.yourbestselfwithdebbie.com

https://www. facebook.com/deborah.salif u

Deborah Lawrence is an emotional and confidence coach who empowers women in their 40s and above to transform their lives from feeling disconnected, lacking direction and

motivation; to reconnect with themselves, experience healing, love, and beauty from within so that they can tap into and unleash their potential for greatness. This was inspired by her journey of finding freedom from past hurts, which had left her with scars, low self-esteem, a poor relationship with herself, and a lack of purpose and motivation for years. She became discontent with her life, started seeking more meaning, and got curious about what was possible. She embarked on a personal development journey that led her to self-discovery, and love, tapping into her gifts. Now she is helping others to do the same.

She is a certified health and life coach by the Health Coach Institute, and accredited

trainer of the Creative Insight Journey (CIJ) - Clarity Catalyst Program, based on a Stanford University Master's degree course. Through this program, she helps her clients become clear on who they are at their core and provides them with practical mindfulness tools and proven emotional intelligence techniques to discover the next powerful chapters in their lives. She also has a degree in Sociology, is certified as a Neurolinguistic Programming Practitioner/Coach, Hypnotherapist, and Timeline Therapist. She uses the skills she acquired in these fields to empower the women she serves to become aware, gain clarity, and learn the skills they need to interrupt self-destructive habits and patterns of self-sabotage, thereby creating more profound and lasting transformations. She has also served in various fields, including banking, technology & communications, fashion, beauty, and working with people with disabilities.

With her passion for fashion and esthetics, she worked as a professional couturier and makeup artist for 18 years, the latter of which she has engaged as a

tool to boost women's confidence instantly. She also uses these skills to help

them break free from mental blocks holding them back so they can rediscover themselves and reignite their passions. She serves as a guide to help her

clients bridge the gap from where they are to where they desire to be so they can live their life to the fullest capacity - tapping into every gift within them to make the beautiful world of their dreams.

As a result of her influence and contributions, she recently received the People's Choice Award from the RAW Leaders Mastermind, amongst a field of

highly successful coaches. In her spare time, she enjoys photography, sings in her local church, and serves others. She believes life is beautiful and should be appreciated so that we can experience it fully. This forms the basis of her existence.

CHAPTER FOUR

THE OTHER SIDE OF DARKNESS

By Deborah Lawrence

She was always strong, courageous, determined, eloquent, resourceful, and creative, with a beautiful soul. She always beamed with joy, her eyes sparkled with so much light, and there was something so charming about her, but life happened. Her precious, memorable moments became history in a heartbeat.

Her life became filled with many twists and turns, mountains, valleys, and wild-fearful storms. She waded through raging storms, alone and scared. Heartbreak, betrayal, rejection, even from loved ones; abuse, abandonment, and physical and mental trauma, were not strangers to her. She needed and sought love, acceptance, comfort, grace, and a strong shoulder she could lean on. She groped in the dark, wondering, "Where do I go from here? What should I do next? What good can ever come out of me? How do I find my way?"

On several occasions, she wondered if she could take those pills and empty the bottle or gather the courage to slice her wrist. If only she could end it all…. At that moment, she realized she could not choose to escape the despair that plagued her as she remembered her mother. How could her mother deal with the pain her little girl had experienced and the loss of her daughter?

Countless times, her weary mind had wondered and doubted she could ever heal. The pain was so excruciating and overwhelming that she felt it was drowning. The depth of the pain words could never fully express; this scar would never fade away, and this memory, time may never erase.

These thoughts filled her mind as she struggled to understand what she had just experienced, and the rest of the journey to her destination felt like the longest drive of her life. She arrived home, received by a loved one who understood the pain and trauma she had just experienced. This loved one stood by her and did not let her drown in the tragedy that had befallen her.

Days, weeks, months, and years passed, but she was still a shadow of herself. She lived through those days, constantly afraid of what could happen or who would hurt her. Every night was as long as forever. Every time she tried to sleep, she awoke to nightmares. Anxiety, depression, and fear became her companions. Her life never remained the same; maybe 'her life would never be the same'?

She had served Him all her life and had not betrayed or let Him down, or so she thought. She was so mad at God because she could not understand why He let her endure this pain. This once bright, cheerful, loving, shining star became a recluse, a shadow of herself, hiding from people, never trusting, never yielding, losing touch with all her friends, and doing everything possible to be unreachable. The pity-partying, isolation, suicidal ideations, sometimes disruptive behaviors, and negative self-talk pushed her deeper into depression and farther away from people.

Considering the emotions that came up due to the pain, and the stigma that society had about victims of such heinous crimes, she could not tell anyone. It remained inside, choking the life out of her while suppressing these emotions until she became numb. She was a prisoner of her thoughts, fears, and emotions. These are the worst prisons of life.

People often want to hang around or be in the same space with others who light them up or create beautiful experiences. Nobody wants a downer or a sad, negative person in their corner for long because we tend to transfer the atmosphere or, as some will say, the energy we carry. Though she received encouragement from those who cared, as long as she had her walls up, she felt helpless, stayed closed off, and chose to remain in that state with negative self-talk and story.

Three years later, she started a new inner dialogue," I cannot continue to be a shadow of myself; I need to heal. I'm tired of feeling broken and being a victim; I'm tired of living my life as a hermit; I'm tired of this voice so loud in my head that it will not allow me to hear anything else." One thing was clear to her; she did not have the necessary tools to help her deal with the after-effect of the event. She also had a deep desire to fill the void and was desperately ready for more, so she got curious.

In her quest to fill this void, she sought answers and help to heal. First, she needed to release and let go of the hurt, then rewrite her narrative of the event and what she thought of herself. She decided it was time and acknowledged the emotions she had tried to numb, choosing forgiveness for those who hurt her.

They did not deserve her forgiveness, and they deserved to rot in hell, but unforgiveness is too heavy a burden to bear, and it weighed her down. She also realized that her healing seemed unachievable as long as her heart stayed closed and unforgiving. She had silently blamed and could not forgive herself for not listening to the still, small voice she had heard in her heart. She struggled with guilt, feeling responsible for what happened to her. Had she not made that trip on that fateful Sunday, had she listened to her pastor, or that little voice inside her that made her hide her little money in a book in case she got robbed, she would not have had this experience. All these questions plagued her thoughts as she struggled for years to survive.

Picking up the pieces left of her was a choice only she could make, and no one else could do that for her. She wished she had decided earlier to embrace her journey, but she could not until she was ready.

She began to ask the Lord to help her heal, knowing that being divinely connected would help her stay grounded. At the same time, she invested in herself by working with a coach who helped her with tools and techniques to help her gain self-awareness and understand and process her emotions. One of her favorite techniques was tapping, where you tap body parts with your fingers while reciting affirmations and desired emotions. This works by reprogramming the mind with a new set of data (the affirmations) to produce new emotions and behavior.

These set her on course for her healing as she yielded herself to do the work necessary, and of course, being a new journey, there were times she failed, but her determination to break free kept her going.

Each time she conversed with the Lord, the relief was quite surprising; she had found a new best friend to tell everything to and still be loved without any judgment. She never realized how powerful forgiveness was. It freed her emotionally, physically, mentally, spiritually, and in every way possible. She realized that life could be beautiful again.

She also saw that she had the power to rewrite her story. She did not have to let her experiences define her. She realized that the abuse had nothing to do with her value or identity; instead, it was about the perpetrators of the crime. Hurt people hurt people. Unfortunately, she had stayed so long, reliving the moments and retelling the stories; the meaning she gave the experience had diminished her perspective of her value.

While on this journey, she needed new thoughts and perspectives to free her from the ones that held her captive. She accomplished this by consciously feeding her mind with information that empowered her to see other rewarding perspectives. The first book she read during this journey was "As a man thinketh by James Allen" which helped her to redirect her thoughts.

One Sunday morning, while at the church, she watched and listened curiously to the sermon as the pastor preached, saying that God is a high priest sensitive to our feelings of infirmity. He knew just what she was feeling, the pain, shame, wounds, and all other emotions she was experiencing. He knew every single emotion she felt.

As the choir sang sweet, soft melodies and harmonies, their voices rising in a beautiful crescendo, the organist, with eyes closed, looking like he was in a trance, played harmoniously; the preacher called out to everyone burdened with care no matter how great or small. "Come home," he said," to everyone feeling bruised and broken, lost and hopeless, lay it all out on the altar before the Lord who is waiting with His arms wide open to give you a love that only He can," he continued. Fragile and vulnerable, trembling, and with tears streaming down her face, she stood and walked down the aisle toward the altar; her arms raised in total surrender to the greatest love she had ever known.

The preacher prayed for her, and she felt a release in her heart, like a bird set free from a cage; her heart felt free from the shame, guilt, blame, and judgment she had held onto for so long. She lost the shackles and received God's peace. It was a kind of calm she had not experienced since the event.

She had always had a deep spiritual connection and the gift of singing, a calling to minister to the Lord, a relationship she had missed and yearned for throughout her dark moments. Gradually she rebuilt that relationship with the Lord through worship and daily conversations. This also helped her to connect with herself. She began to feel empowered because she was starting to embrace her purpose again.

In no time, the strength returned, the vision became clearer again, and it was as if she had walked onto a stage with all the lights on. She could see again! There was a light at the end of this tunnel.

The star received light to shine again! This light shone so brightly upon everyone around her. She learned to trust God daily for a brand-new mercy and experienced the power of forgiveness given to others and oneself.

Now, she gets a blank canvas to rewrite her story to herself and the world. Whom she becomes depends on what she chooses to continue to create. A new identity.

Each time she listened to mind-blowing, thought-provoking training, she got a new perspective that helped her shift her old mindset from "this happened to me" to "this happened for me," she felt even more empowered.

Tony Robbins significantly influenced her and inspired her to study Neuro-Linguistic Programming. He always talked about how giving experiences a new meaning impacts thought processes and eventually determines behaviors in those situations. Giving her experiences new meanings and changing how she looked at things gave her much hope and courage to see what was possible. It also became easier for her to take each next step needed.

It was time to transition from surviving to thriving, dreaming, playing, and engaging with friends again. She returned to work and turned all that energy into creating results, reigniting her passions, tapping into all her gifts, and making her dreams come true. In addition to her work, she is also a public speaker and serves in her church. She is fully aware of how powerful she is, has found her voice, and is living her life unapologetically.

Life is always full of undulations, highs, lows, connections, memories, adventures, accidents, and tragedies, all of which make life interesting. The twists and turns build us. Imagine life with no new learning experiences, no happy and sad times, and no fights with siblings and friends; life as we know it would be so bland.

On the other side of darkness, there is always a ray of hope and sunshine. If we can quiet ourselves to listen to and follow the voice inside, that voice can lead us to light, where we can find hope, purpose, and praise.

Five lessons I learned from her story are:

1) Give yourself permission to get help. You can handle things independently, but the struggle is real when trying to do it alone.
2) Taking responsibility to create the desired change, needs courage.

3) Your mind is so powerful. When you change how you look at things, the things you look at change.
4) Recognize the stories you tell yourself. It can liberate you or keep you stuck.
5) Quiet yourself, listen to, and follow your inner voice.

Let's do a check-in.

Do you resonate with her story?

....

Where are you on your journey

....

Here is a little exercise on how to overcome trauma.

Important steps must be taken to overcome trauma; when this is done, you can regain your power.

1) Make a choice
2) Know who you are
3) The power of reframing your perspective.
4) Invest in yourself,
5) Connect with your passions

1) Make a choice.

Things will always happen in life. Some of these events will happen by chance, and others you plan for, but you get to choose how it impacts you, and your choice is your voice. It is your life, and as the director of the movie of your life, you have the power to create a happy ending, as a painter, you can splash colors on your new canvas, making it as beautiful as you desire, as a writer, you get to rewrite your story on a new blank page, and if you are a

singer, you get to sing a new song with fresh notes, rhythms, harmonies, genre, name it.

You can always decide to let the impact of your experiences make or mar you.

Choose what you want, how you want it, when, and where you want it, and then take the necessary steps to make it happen. Choose you!

Where have you given up your choice?

What are you choosing in that situation?

Whom are you choosing?

2) **Know who you are and who you are not.**

You are not the circumstance!

Even if something terrible happened, it does not define you.

You are worthy irrespective of the experience. The feelings and emotions that come with it can cloud your view of who you truly are.

Now Make a list of what makes you unique.

What lights you up?

Whom do you want to show up as?

Who are you on your happiest days?

How do you express yourself on your happiest days?

Now that is who you really are.

3) Reframe your perspective.

Reframing means changing the meaning you attach to things. It shifts your perspectives, changes your feelings about the situation, and builds creativity. You become a problem solver and handle situations more resourcefully.

What meaning have you attached to a situation that no longer serves you?

Where else have you taken things personally that hurt you but really weren't yours to carry?

Can you possibly feel different about the situation?

How else can the situation be resolved?

Imagine that time and money were not an issue, what do you desire to create in the future?

4) Invest in yourself.

Invest in yourself. Yes, you are valuable!

An investment in your personal development equips and builds you up for life. You build the best of you as you shed and let go of things, habits, beliefs, relationships, jobs, and other entanglements that no longer serve you so that you can become like gold tried in the fire and having lost its impurities, it shines in its purest form.

Where can you invest in yourself today?

What can you invest in yourself today?

How can you invest in yourself today?

5) Connect with your passions.

Passion comes from the heart, not the head. It is something you lose track of because you love and enjoy it. Chances are, you already know your passion and may need to connect with it.

What is your passion?

How do you connect with it?

Are you doing that today?

Make a list of things you love to do and set out a time to do them.

Acknowledge your strengths and achievements.

Dr. NASRIN (NAS) PARSIAN

"To Change the World, tap on to your heart! It is not about discovering who you are but Creating who you truly are."
-Dr. Nas Parsain

Holistic and Emotional Health Consultant and Educator, Academic Nurse, HB-NLP, and Hypnotherapy Trainer
info@drnasinnerwellness.com
www.drnasinnerwellness.com

Dr. Nasrin (Nas) Parsian is a Holistic health professional, Academic Nurse, and Emotional health Consultant, experienced for 25 years in a wide range of health and wellness paradigms, Evidence-Based Practice in healthcare, Pediatrics, children and youth well-being, chronic illnesses management, and her highest passion is on Spirituality, Self-transformation, and Health. She holds a PhD, from Deakin University Melbourne, Australia, on spirituality and self-transformation in people with chronic health conditions, focusing on diabetes-type one. The results of the project revealed the significance of self-transformation in management of chronic illnesses and were very well received by many national and international scientific conferences and peer reviewed journals. In her research project, she applied both qualitative and quantitative methodologies and developed the validated SQ questionnaire that is being used by psychology and health related students in their projects.

Nasrin's latest and most powerful interest is Heart Intelligence, coherent neuro-transformation and inner wellness.

Nas has a strong background in teaching, research, and higher education in university, curriculum development, and clinical practice. She is also a Neuro-Linguistics Programming (NLP) and hypnotherapy master practitioner and trainer, transformational coaching educator, a member of American Board of Hypnotherapy (ABH), and a contributor author in eYs International Humanitarian Magazine.

Dr. Parsian is a founder of her own consulting, training, and coaching business operating as "Dr. Nas Inner Wellness," currently practicing as a consultant and educator for holistic and emotional health and educating professionals about the relevant tools/approaches, while working as an academic in nursing and midwifery discipline in Australia. Her vision adheres to an holistic approach for people's inner wellness with the focus on Heart-Based transformation.

She offers on-line training and coaching programs, a podcast, certification training programs, coherent neuro-transformation, and heart-centered health. Her signature training and mentoring program, Conscious Heart-Based Coaching (CHBC), offers two certifications of HB-NLP practitioner and Hypnotherapy practitioner.

Nasrin's strongest passion is to help people achieve their optimal physical and emotional well-being through the process of coherent transformation and connectedness with Inner Self and Heart intelligence. Her consulting areas focus on self-transformation, mental/emotional health, stress, anxiety, trauma, burnout, youth emotional health, resilience, and self-empowerment. She believes the heart has a leading role in transformation and inner wellness.

Dr. Parsian leads people to discover their higher purpose and create new meaning in any given situation and helps them break state through empowerment and connectedness with the 'whole', communicating with the inner intelligence. She is helping people become aware of their health in deeper layers, unfold the unknown areas, become the master of their wellness, and ultimately create their newness.

Nasrin has a compassionate personality with a higher purpose and passion to uplift and inspire humans to evolve to their best 'Self,' connect to the heart, and recreate their inner wellness and fuller life. Her own several transformational journeys of cocoon breaking and her deep connection to the ancient mystics of Rumi and the concept of ONENESS enlighten her insight of harmonious and heart-centered health.

Education Background

PhD in Spirituality, Self-Transformation and Diabetes type 1 management.

Master of Pediatrics Nursing

Bachelor of Nursing Science- RNGrad Cert in Higher Education

Certified NLP Master Practitioner and Trainer

Certified Hypnotherapy Master Practitioner and Trainer

CHAPTER FIVE

SECOND OPINION: WELLNESS IS AN INSIDE JOB!

by Dr Nasrin (Nas) Parsian,

"My physical body is a temple of the living spirit, which animates it, rebuilds it after the image of its own perfection, and keeps it in perfect health, harmony, and wholeness." Ernest Holmes

We hear, see, and feel these days so many unresolved problems in human's health and wellness. What is really happening in our world? Twenty percent of teenagers have depression. Dementia has been reported even in young adults. Chronic illnesses, auto-immune diseases, cancer, cardiovascular conditions, mental health issues are becoming the skyrocket.

Where are we now? Where are we going? Where is our health going?

As a health professional for over two decades, in work from clinical nursing to undertaking various research projects, teaching many different health-care related subjects, and running an inner wellness business, I was always impressed by the strong links between a whole person, the mind and heart contexts and how they impact our lives and health. To me, humans are not simply a product of the biological revolution that happened hundreds of thousands of years ago. Humans are deeply connected to a 'Whole'.

Today's biomedical and conventional model of health to fix the "human" is missing something! Because they are limited to correcting just the biochemistry of our cells. Not to mention that these models basically aim to only save the human nation from dying rather than healing for better and quality living. So, their goal is more about surviving rather than thriving. As a result, people's quality of life in all areas is increasingly declining, the root causes remain unattended, and the healing solutions are not sustainable.

This massive gap in our mainstream healthcare system is causing more health problems, both physically and emotionally/mentally. Chronic illnesses are not well managed, and the numbers keep going up every day. Mental and emotional health issues do not respond to the quick fix approaches, so they become more complicated. What is missing here?

It is the best and worst time now in history to transform your health and wellness and evolve to your new YOU. You might have been fighting for long or even for so many years with unwanted situations that affected your well-being emotionally/ mentally, and physically. You might have been misdiagnosed or mistreated by polypharmacy with no ultimate results. You might have experienced a traumatic situation, a loss, grief, or uncontrollable chronic stress with a massive unresolved long-term impact on your life and well-being.

The bad news is that everything in our world is becoming a commercial, superficial, transnational structure and rarely is about the heart. But the good news is humans like you and I are now seeking accountability to create a meaningful transformation, explore and understand the barriers that enable emotional well-being. The purpose is indeed optimizing emotional wellness to open the gateway to becoming your better Self and, consequently, a healthier life.

Humanity is a "Whole" needing to be nurtured with an integrated approach to come to an aligned inner balance. This inner balance leads to harmoniously integrated wholeness not by telling people what to do, rather by self-empowerment and facilitating the softening process of wakefulness and heartfulness.

Wholeness or Oneness is a concept of universal consciousness. The energy in each atom has a consciousness, comprising our perception, and is connected to the energy emitted by other atoms in the universe. The energy in our body is intertwined with our inner intelligence. The universe is a unity of energy where everything is connected and cannot be divided into separate pieces. For example, Black and white are not separate entities; they are parts of a single gradient composed of a billion different shades of gray.

It is all about ONENESS. New science of epigenetics is revolutionizing a link between mind and matter. As soon as we deviate the focus from a perception of a "whole," from the heart, from the soul to the matter, we begin to experience separation. Our nervous system then functions based on the received signals, and our DNA is coded by the downloaded programs linked to the membrane perceptions. Every single cell has membranes that receive the signals, and every signal impacts the cells' behavior and eventually people's health.

Before reading through this chapter, I like you to answer the following questions:

1. Can you confidently and regularly communicate with your thoughts, emotions, and body? If yes, how?

2. Did you know that your wellness is so much about an embodied coherence and integration as a 'whole'? What does it really mean to you?
3. You are healthy when All of You is integrated emotionally, psychologically, socially, and physically.

In this chapter, you will read about:

- *The ONE cause of dis-ease*
- *What can we do*
- *Change begins with you*
- *HEART is the leader*
- *A model of Coherent Wellness and the HEARTFUL formula*

The ONE cause of dis-ease

My whole personal and professional life brought me to a conclusion that the One cause of the majority of mental and physical conditions is ongoing STRESS, which is unfortunately not getting thorough attention in our healthcare system. We talk or hear about stress all the time, but practically we do nothing about it. What is stress, and how does it impact our body's functions? Let's just unfold it a bit.

Stress is generally a way by which the body overcomes a demanding or undesirable situation, as sometimes it might not be undesirable. For example, if someone is going to experience an adventure, which is stressful, it's something that they chose; it's not an undesirable or unwanted situation, but see this is stressful, and this kind of stress brings some thrilled and joyful excitement.

Stress is indeed natural where your body reacts to a different situation. So, whenever you are in a different and unknown situation, your body tries to maintain a balance, maintain the homeostasis, and protect itself from the attack of the unknown or emergency alarm. Stress is indeed a series of events that your body follows to adapt with those situations. This is sometimes called acute or situational stress. It's short-term, coming and going very quickly. And generally, it's recognised with symptoms such as anger, anxiety, and sometimes acute periods of depression.

If it occurs very often and frequently, then it is called episodic stress. Some people experience it due to a series of stressful and challenging situations they are carrying in their lives, one after the other, especially when they go through a very stressful life transition or so. When stress persists for a longer period, then it's called chronic stress, which can cause disease and illness. So, let's just do not forget that the key is the body's response. So, the stress is not bad by itself; the body's response is key.

Your body is indeed functioning to save you, save itself. So, the stages of the body's response start with an initial alarm, then adaptation, and finally recovery or, if the recovery doesn't happen, exhaustion. The alarm is the very first stage, which is involved basically with fight and flight responses. Fight or flight is the job of the autonomic nervous system. Body is getting prepared either to face the perceived threat or to escape from it.

There are Central Nervous System (CNS) and Peripheral Nervous System (PNS) in human's body. So, the central nervous system has indeed the main responsibility to make the order. CNS consists of the brain and spinal cord. So, all body sensations and changes in our external environment, or received from the receptors and sense organs, go to the CNS to be interpreted.

The second part is the peripheral nervous system, which is indeed carrying all the messages from periphery to the central nervous system. The Peripheral Nervous System has two subdivisions, the sensory system, including all sensory neurons that carry information from receptors in the periphery of the body to the brain and spinal cord, and the motor system, carrying information from the brain and the spinal cord to muscles and glands motor system; which can be further subdivided into two subcategories, somatic nervous system, conducting impulses from the brain and spinal cord to skeletal muscle and causing us to respond or react to changes in our environment. The second branch of the motor system is the Autonomic Nervous System (ANS), which conducts impulses from the brain and spinal cord to smooth muscle tissue, cardiac muscle tissues, and glands.

ANS is considered to be involuntary. So, it means its function is automatic. That means, you know, we do not think about what is happening as a result of autonomic nervous system function. You do not think about how your heart is beating. You do not think about how the lungs are functioning and how the breathing process. You do not think, and you don't have any control on the gastrointestinal system to digest your foods. You don't think about how the food is just passing through the digestive system to the intestine and bowel. So, there is no thinking about any stages of body function, which are under control of your autonomic nervous system. So the organs are affected by this system, receiving a nerve from two divisions, sympathetic division and parasympathetic division; sympathetic division speeds up activity, and parasympathetic division speeds down activities. So, one is stimulating, and the other one is indeed slowing down.

So, when the fire alarm gets pulled, sympathetic division causes some reactions into your body as a result of stress, hormones, cortisol, and noradrenaline, and adrenaline from adrenal glands; for example, increased heart rate, rise in blood sugar level, high or sometimes low blood pressure and some gastrointestinal dysfunctions. If the body can adapt to the situation, the recovery may happen in five minutes or so, a maximum of 20 minutes. So if the body's competencies, compensation, or mechanisms do not act successfully, then the signs and symptoms can eventually affect the whole system in the body. One of the most important systems affected by the situation is the immune system.

In an emergency state, a message goes out from the brain to the immune system to stop the immune system from functioning and put the immune system on hold. Why would the brain sensor send a message to the immune system? Because it wants to save your life. Your immune system is consuming a lot of energy, and fight, and flight function also is consuming a lot of energy. Which one is more urgent in this situation? The body recognises the emergency attack is more serious and it is going to survive in that situation. Because if the body doesn't survive, the whole organs in the body can be affected by stress hormones. So, this is an urgent situation, and the body needs to preserve their energy just to handle that situation. Therefore, it puts the immune system on hold and just deals with that situation until it is safe. There is no serious problem if it takes five minutes or so. But if it takes longer or happens very frequently, then what would be the outcome? It will certainly lead to a serious illness. On the other hand, you keep your immune system on hold. You know that a lot of health problems are indirectly or directly involved with immune system functionality, such as cancer. So, you actually expose the body to cancer with chronic or unresolved stress.

Basically, the conventional medical system is advising people to take the medication or use the quick fix approach that might work well in the emergency situation. While it may temporarily alleviate the symptoms, the solution is not sustainable and, at times, may cause other problems in our bodies. Stress needs to be healed.

Sometimes we experience stress, or its symptoms, which are not even related to the real environmental event and could be just something related to your thoughts and past experiences, and emotions; that is discussed under the category of imaginative stress, which is the topic of another discussion.

Therefore, stress healing is certainly involved with some deep work with your subconscious mind, your nervous system, and, more profoundly, your heart. It cannot be healed simply by medication, quick fix approaches or our logics and analytical thinking, cognitive therapy, or merely by relaxation techniques. While you may be able to manage it for a while using the above mentioned approaches, you may connect automatically to your past memories in some situations that could be destructive in the long term.

Fear, shame, and guilt are coming from very past stored memories just to save you. You cannot do anything about this when you are not aware of those things. So, in the right process, deeper layers need to come to your awareness. Your body hard drive and programming, energy, and the power of the heart are all involved in the process of healing.

We understand now that stress can be the one cause of dis-eases, both mentally and physically, when it is not resolved and when it occurs frequently. Stress does affect the signals in the body that are carried to the hypothalamus and activate ANS to fight and flight. When they continue, they can hold the immune system from functioning and can come with frequent, undesirable, and unhealthy symptoms that eventually may end up with a disease.

Sometimes stress is internal or related to the cellular memories, and you are not aware of them.

So, a sustainable solution is coming with whatever you can do to disrupt the signal's movement to the nervous system.

What can we do?

"If peace is really what you want, then you need to really choose peace! If peace matters to you more than anything else and if you truly knew your-self to be spirit, you would remain non-reactive and absolutely alert when confronted with challenging situations." Eckhart Tolle

Here I'm going to use TRANSFORM as an acronym to give some tips; so it can be used as a guide to deal with stress and chronic anxiety in a therapeutic way and make peace for your mind, body, and heart.

Let's start with "T". Trust is the very first step to begin any journey. Before you start applying any practices or guides in your life, you need to communicate with your heart and reassure that you TRUST!

Talk loudly and say: "I trust my Heart ."You need to trust yourself first to be able to go through the process of Self-awareness and Self-healing, and only then are you able to notice what is happening in your body, in your mind, in your heart; only then you are able to notice your emotions; and you're begin-ning to notice your patterns whether you 'React' or 'Respond' to a situation.

Reading reactivity is the second step. The moment you begin to judge your-self, you are no longer reading reactivity. So just be careful that you're not judgemental. You are basically your best self-observant. When you notice you're holding back from what you want to say or you're not sure how to approach the topic, you are reading and observing your reactivity. If you start to judge the person or the situation or make a story in your mind about it in advance or keep telling yourself of how badly you feel, then you are not an observer. So, rather than focusing on what you did or what you said, I encourage you to observe your reactivity level.

Notice the quality of your thoughts and communicate with your emotions. So, the more fearful your thoughts, the higher the level of reactivity. When you are aware of what is happening around, how you feel, how you express yourself and your emotions, you're less reactive. When you just try to find fault in yourself or others, you indeed hold back from expressing your emotions. When you are not able to stay focused on a specific task or forget your everyday things, you are at a high level of reactivity. You can give a number out of 10 to your reactivity to make your awareness a bit more tangible.

Awareness comes next. Awareness is always a key for any kind of growth and any kind of management in the context of health and well-being.

Figure 1: Johari's Window of Self-Awareness

I like how Johari's windows simply clarified the areas of Self-awareness. While I got so impressed the first time I learned about this model, I love to discuss the concept of Self-awareness in further depth and go beyond the cognitive level.

Let's first take your attention here to the differences between Self-reflection and Self-awareness. Self-reflection is more a mental experience. It is more following thoughts, while Self-awareness is rather bodily experience, focusing on emotions and bodily sensations, and feeling. For example, you are witnessing your breath; you are feeling your own body and your body feedback, your body sensations. Self-reflection is more about self-study and self-learning, but self-awareness is more about self-practice. Self-reflection is usually a reflection happening in the moment, but self-awareness is basically appreciation of the moment, but it is ongoing, it's not limited to the time.

When you actually reflect on your emotions, it is self-reflection, so you can identify your emotions. But in Self-awareness, you go further and beyond, you feel the emotions, you feel the sensations of those emotions in your body and your heart. For example, when you feel sad, what do you feel in your heart? What do you feel in your gut? What do you feel in other parts of your body? You need to feel those sensations while you still can use your thoughts and write them down in self-reflection. You feel your thoughts, you feel your feelings!

You can only reset your nervous system and your vagus nerve, and your autonomic nervous system when you go through the self-awareness practice comfortably and frequently because you need to feel comfortable with your body to be able to reset your body and your nervous system.

I did self-reflection for nearly my whole life, but to be honest, I couldn't make deep changes in my body, nervous system, and well-being until I started deeply communicating with my body centered in the heart. I basically provided the environment and the situation that my nervous system is going through the process of reset by itself with no real additional effort.

You need to look inwardly. Listen to what your inner voice is telling you at this moment. How do you really feel in your body, in your heart? List any sensations that can be felt, heavy, warm, cool, tight, tense, or open pressure. When you notice your sensations, you can communicate with your deep emotions. Take a moment to try this, sit on a chair, place your feet flat on the floor. Sit with an intention like you're going to make a speech, visualize your spine without moving your head or shoulders, notice your breath, and communicate with your body. You can feel how you place your attention on your sensation and how you begin to settle into your self-awareness. I would like to suggest, for your breath, to prolong your exhale because in any exhale, to be able to balance your parasympathetic nerve function, which is the calming part of the autonomic nervous system.

'Nerve reset' is the result of awareness. You can reset the vagus nerve, which is the longest nerve in the body and the most important nerve in the parasympathetic system. To be able to do this, place the index finger of your right hand above your navel, then press to the right and inward. Put three fingers of your left hand at the top of your head at the back, then press your fingers, the middle of your skull at the top of your head, and then to the front, just about your forehead. Do the process simultaneously with one hand pressing points just about the navel and the other hand pressing the top of your head; repeat this process several times. You will notice your breath becomes deeper, your jaw, neck, and shoulders feel looser, and you get fairly relaxed. If you didn't notice that, do it again.

'Sync' your breath with your heart. It is called a coherence between breath and your heart.

Previously medical science thought that the heart should be really regularly working like a metronome. But evidence shows now that the heart is not a metronome. The healthy heart doesn't have to be like a metronome and just beats regularly with the same interval. Heart Rate Variability (HRV) is now a measure used to assess the heart-breath or heart-brain coherence in the body. If your heartbeat is not regular, it is because your heart is just trying to protect you based on the situations you're facing too. So, if you are facing a stressful situation, your heart starts to beat faster and irregularly, and that's a protective function. However, you're not going to stay in that protection function. Are you? That's why you need to take any charge action to make a coherence between your breath and your heart. Heart focused breathing can ease heart rhythm and sync your breath with heart. As you continue a heart-focused breathing, try to experience a newly generated feeling such as appreciation, care, love for someone or something in your life. So, you need to practice these things very often, again and again, and focus on a feeling of calm and ease. Synchronizing your breath with your heart at the beginning might not be easy. You can start with the specific technique of 10 seconds, four seconds breath in, and six seconds breath out. It's going to be 10 seconds all together for one breathing cycle. So, you can start practicing rhythmically in 10 seconds fashion until you feel more comfortable with your heart rhythm. At the same time, focus on your positive emotions and visualize something nice, a nice place, a nice loving story, or a good past experience, a person who you love, whatever it can give you a calm and peaceful, and loving feeling. And once you feel more comfortable with that feeling, concentrate on your heart rhythm and sync your breath with that state. It is important to stop analytical or abstract thinking. Thinking indeed increases your brain activity, and that is exactly what you don't want. The brain activity increases the neural-cortex activity and eventually increases the level of cortisol.

'Food' is definitely the one that we should not forget. Yes. Food! It's very important because the gut in your body is a significant part of your autonomic nervous system regulation. Because the vagus nerve is centered in your gut.

Your gut is also responsible for producing serotonin. Evidence discusses that if you suffer from depression and anxiety, or your moodiness retainability, you need to consider creating a healthy lifestyle that supports your gut. So that's why I suggest before starting anything, to heal or deal with stress, you need to manage what you eat and start consuming healthy foods, whole foods and hydrate your body. Just get more natural and less processed food, lean organic meats, coconut or almond milk instead of cow milk, fruit, calcium, vegetables with high antioxidants, foods high in dopamine, like bananas, dark chocolate, turmeric. I would suggest you get in touch with amazing people who are working on nutrition, revolution, ethically functional nutrition, functional medicine, and you will be surprised by so much information to make your body healthier in terms of eating. This is opening a healthy communication with your body; basically, body talk. Learn the skills of asking questions and receiving answers from your body.

'Open your body dialogue'. This follows the previous stage. When you communicate with another person, you're often noticing the nonverbal language, the body expression, and their words as feedback. But when you communicate with your body, you are noticing basically the sensations and feelings in you.

Through this process, you can fully understand what the gaps or triggers are. I can find every day a lot of triggers, a lot of gaps, a lot of areas in myself that need work. And I need to address it through talking to my body, what she is clearly speaking to me about.

I usually ask loudly: How do you feel right now?

Through opening this dialogue, you can notice and feel the suppressed energy, suppressed emotions, and suppressed beliefs. Energy, emotions, and beliefs are the keys for a better life. The purpose of this communication is to allow the unhealed wounds to become obvious and evident. Then you're able to transport those and heal them to the next stage.

Release! Here is when you can again use the breathing techniques. Start with smooth breathing for 10 to 15 seconds; when you're ready, you can do powerful deep breathing, like prana breathing and Heart-focused breathing.

Your jaw is an important part of your body here that needs releasing. Because the jaw is the connector between the lower parts of energy in the body, the core sections, and the upper parts of the energy. Your jaw also affects your throat energy center, and can be considered the bridge between your heart and mind. So, blocking this bridge can constrain the energy.

You can release your jaw through an exhale from the abdominal area and bring the energy from the core side up to the brain. This pattern takes you to a relaxed and peaceful level of consciousness that promotes your healing.

'Meditate!' Meditation, Self-hypnosis, or some techniques of Neuro-Linguistic Programming like anchoring do not have to have a spiritual aim. The entire aim of using these techniques is just simply to shift your brain from to a harmonious calmness. You don't have to be in an alpha state of the brain to do this practice. So, you can just do it within everyday active life using the heart-focused breathing. The heart is so powerful, and the electromagnetic field of the heart is 60 times stronger than the brain's fields. Focusing on your heart in your meditation, Self-hypnosis of NLP exercises will strengthen your connection with your 'Inner Self.'

During your practice, I would suggest you put your hand on your heart, sync your breath with your heart, speak to your heart, ask your heart to bring more and deeper love to your body. The problem in the process of healing is more about the energy, and the energy of the heart intelligence is super strong, and it is the best source to use to recover your energy.

Change begins with YOU.

Most of us are influenced by our families and society to follow paths and programs that we are instructed to do. So, our roles and important decisions are often conditioned because we are told we "Should" rather than we "feel or desire," so they might not be a fit for who we truly are. As a result, we may not live a life with genuine purpose aligned with our natural talents, interests, and who you truly are. This was one of my biggest barriers in my growth journey, and took me years of inner work to be able to free myself from those conditions and programs.

Changes begin where we realize the misalignment, when we realize something is not really right! There will certainly be curvy roads, valleys, lakes, seas, mountains, forests, deserts waiting for you in this path. The clearer knowledge and insight, the more powerful you become to move on this path.

When you become aware of your consciousness, you will learn how to track the flow of the energy in your whole body and let it flow within your whole "YOU ." Here is where you begin transforming to an integrated and coherent YOU.

Reflective Questions

- Do I live in alignment with my true/inner Self?
- Do I feel limited or lacking something, or do I feel complete as a whole?
- Am I attached to my limiting beliefs or empowering beliefs?
- Do I feel 'Me' as a whole, sensing my body, heart, mind, spirit all as ONE?

We have two choices in life: allow all the unexpected or negative aspects of life to be a curse or turn them into blessings and gifts to grow. When we see experiences as an opportunity, we start to see differently, and even the hardest obstacles and challenges turn out to be the biggest possibility to grow. Some events in our lives lead us to such meaningful situations that we can't help but see how they are really leading us toward something greater!

This vision is profoundly important for your health and wellness journey, where you see clearly the two endpoints of the spectrum from extreme pain to the flourishing joy. Your role, responsibility, and action are to create a dynamic integration and flow in this situation.

Siegel (2010) highlights the healthy system is a system that somehow maintains integration and complexity and avoids the extremes of rigidity and chaos. Elaborating upon the metaphor of the river, Siegel asks us to consider rigidity and chaos as the left and right bank of the river, respectively. The ideal position for the self-organizing person is in the center of the river—in the flow—where matter and energy move freely and where there is scope to maximize complexity and integration. The central flow of the river is the place where the five FACES of optimal health and well-being can flourish. An integrated system is marked by a Flexible, Adaptive, Coherent, Energised, and Stable (FACES) flow (Siegel 2010).

Reflective Questions:

- What is involved with my true health?
- What are my emotions, and how are they related to my health?
- What is, in general, my vision about life and my wellbeing?
- What do I need to be able to live healthy and fully?
- How responsible am I to transform my own wellness?

Remember, we all share a universal consciousness; all of us are connected. Thus, we magnify oneness energy when entering a relationship with someone. Your energy creates energetic cord entanglements from anywhere in the universe, and it's intertwined with your inner DNA as well as every single particle in the universe.

Wholeness and connectedness are at the core of human's ultimate wellness and transformation. You cannot achieve your optimized well-being and your best version unless you genuinely CONNECT with your body, your whole being, and with the whole world.

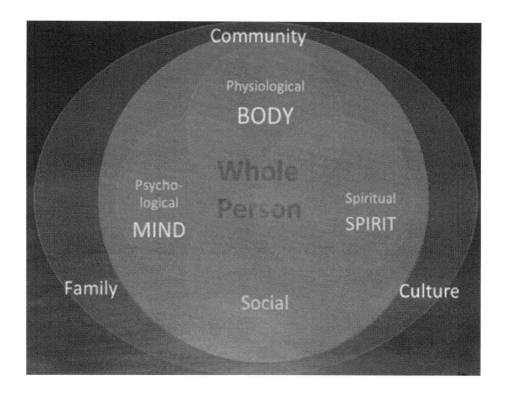

Figure 2: Model of Wholeness depicted from Spirituality conceptual framework (Parsian, N. 2009)

Exercise reflective Questions:

- Am I connected to the whole, or am confused and disconnected?
- Do I feel connected with the present moment?
- Do I have fulfilling relationships with my world and people around?
- Am I feeling connected with the energy of nature?
- Do I socially feel loving, safe, and connected, or do I feel lonely and fearful?

Heart is the leader!

In this process, the heart has a significant leading role. By ignoring the connection between the heart, body, and the mind, with the heart leading the way, we are continuing to lack the quality of care we need for our body to heal and recover. We know that all human beings yearn to feel a sense of connection and purpose, and when we do, our body's healing process speeds up.

By connecting to the heart-intelligence, we discover a deep awareness of what's emotionally inside of the heart. The brain function is very important, but the new science now shows the brain receives many signals from the heart.

Heart-centered integrated health focuses on the idea that our beliefs are affected by and tightly interrelated to our emotions. Most people say it's the other way around, that we need to "control our emotions with our mind or our thoughts ."In other words, when we do control our emotions with our thoughts, they become buried in our body. Therefore, they become stronger and in the long term they are being carried and perceived as signals to the cells' membrane and DNA, causing disease, physically, mentally, or both. On the other hand, being open and inviting to reunite with the whole, and the heart intelligence in the center, helps people connect with the deeply rooted emotions and thoughts, become self-aware, communicate with emotions for the purpose of sustainable healing.

Health professionals and practitioners mostly do not have a deep awareness of what is emotionally inside of their patients' heart. I believe that's why our healthcare fails. From a genuine holistic perspective and in our medical practice, the body, the gut, the head, and heart must be aligned, they must be coherent, and from there, integrated plans can be put into place to help people onto the road of recovery, healing, and enhanced well-being. The heart is the center to lead this coherence. The moment we create a connection with something bigger, higher, more powerful, our heart beats change, and the healing begins!

Integrating the human's intelligences leading with the heart intelligence in our healthcare system will bring a new perspective that can shift DNA, increase better health outcomes, and revolutionize our mainstream health-care system as a whole!

The Model of Coherent Inner Wellness and the HEARTFUL formula

Relying on strategies that deviate to face up to the root causes may result in changing the un-ease into another form that can be just tolerable for a while but eventually fade away or turn to become a new problem.

The Model of Coherent Inner Wellness (MCIW) is created to be used to follow the wellness journey from awareness to unfolding the deep causes, transforming and ultimately achieving the expected alignment and wholeness.

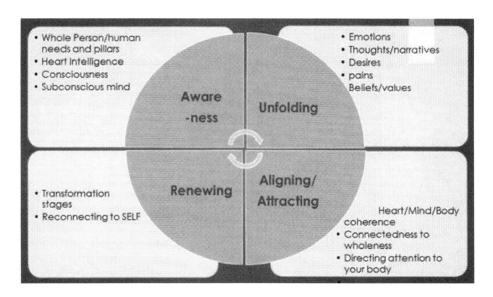

Figure 3: Model of Coherent Inner Wellness

Coherent Awareness, Unfolding, Renewing, Alignment (AURA) cycle can help with our evolutionary challenge to awaken our sensitivity to our emotions, connections, and our wholeness. Heart in this journey facilitates our return to holistic body intelligence rather than technology-structured divisions. Finding the essence of your consciousness and awakening connections with your heart will literally CHANGE your life and optimize your inner wellness!

I like to introduce the practical eight-steps HEARTFUL formula that has helped myself and my clients move through the above cycle and cohere their mind and nervous system with the heart. The experience may feel a bit difficult in your first trial, but you will be surprised how this is going to be more exciting, joyful, and it's kind of addicting in a good way. You will eventually find yourself to be your own bus driver and In-Charge of who you 'Are' and who you are 'Becoming.'

Step 1: *Healing Triangle*

Learn about the healing triangle, which focuses on the three angles:

1) Your healing body, which is basically working with your immune system to protect your health and well-being
2) Dealing with the One cause of dis-ease: Stress
3) Your heart, which is the powerful source to restore your healing body and optimize your immune system's function.

So, before every practice, remember that these three principles need to be the focus of every health process.

Step 2: *Embodied Heart Intelligence- The harmonious Coherence*

Heart knows all the answers to your better Self and your well-being needs once you understand how to connect harmoniously. Heart intelligence is powerfully leading this harmony. Breathing techniques and heartful meditation are some of the important and efficient techniques to facilitate this embodiment. In this step, begin with heart-focused breathing practice and connect more to your emotions. Stop judging if your emotions are good or bad and instead begin to care for them, like a mother caring for her baby.

Step 3: *Awareness (Deeper awareness)*

Your inner wellness is closely involved with an integrated inner approach, and that is not possible unless you achieve an expanded self-awareness. Who you are, and what does it involve with a person as a Whole? Your awareness goes beyond the multifaceted pillars in your whole being. This is the key to begin the journey of transforming your wellness. In your awareness practice, focus on your Thoughts, Emotions, and Desires (TEDs) and how they can be connected to achieve optimal functions in your body. In this step, you will learn about your conscious, subconscious, and unconscious mind, the differences, and how to deal with them. Apply what we discussed in the awareness section.

Step 4: *Redefining situations, Beliefs/values - Meaning making*

This is a very important step! Choose to rise above your pre-built beliefs stored in your subconscious mind and create new ones. Once you begin to dive within and question yourself and your life with the term "Why Me," know that you stepped into a bigger creation. Start to search for any possible solutions to find a new approach in the given scenario. This stage is usually so hard, and you may swing several times between past and present. Redefining is a very significant stage for a transformational journey. I would suggest reading the Man's Search for Meaning by Victor Frankl and dare to live by MEANING.

Step 5: Transformation

This stage is where the true process of transformation happens. Old beliefs, values, and framework are replaced by the new ones. Begins by building up the New meaning from the depth of ashes and dark layers you had dived in the previous steps. In this step, you affirm and practice the three Cs as many times as you can: CHOOSE the path of healing, COMMIT to begin the journey, CREATE a new meaning that will lead to transforming your wellness.

Step 6: Flourish your present and future 'Self'

Do we need to relive the past stories to achieve becoming a better self? Well, my answer is no! In this step, reflect on the present moment and what you want to be in your future moment. Be comfortable with your present Self and be clear about your future Self and your purpose. Watch and listen to all the possible images and voices. You will then formulate plans to achieve the new Self.

Step 7: Ultimate your sense of alignment

In this step, you are embodying your whole being and making things real. Your well-being is when you align your thoughts, emotions, nervous system, and bodily signals all as one. You have a clearer understanding about the function of the autonomic system and how it can be easily manipulated by your thoughts and emotions. Your bodily sensations give you some valid information and evidence about these connections. You follow using the tools that align these connections and assess or evaluate it by the evidence of sensations and biological manifestations. In this step, you will start to personalize your needs, including your healthy lifestyle and eating needs, based on what you create and what is in alignment with your whole being. This is only the beginning, and it's an ongoing process that needs constant practice and further learning.

Step 8: *Luminate New You*

In this final step, review your clear vision and purpose for your life and well-being. You will discover your sense of Self, what lights you and your well-being up. You dissolve any limiting self-beliefs or fears and improve your relationship with yourself and others.

You reclaim health and harmony in your life, communicate lovingly with your emotions, feel your body sensations and the biological responses to stress and calmness, and maintain a healthy connection with your whole being. You are a master of your emotional state in challenging situations and live in alignment with your heart intelligence. You are confident to step out of your comfort zone and openly create any new changes needed.

Enjoy the amazing journey!

Leonie FEAST-JONES

https://feastonlife.com.au/

leonie@feastonlife.com.au

Leonie Feast-Jones is a pioneer in the field of energy healing with international exposure. For over 30 years she has been transforming the lives of individuals and reinvigorating organizations. Highly skilled and certified in a wide range of healing and coaching modalities, Leonie has developed a unique and fully integrated energy healing technique that empowers and inspires individuals to become more aware of their insecurities or relevant issues that are limiting their ability to move forward with greater positivity.

The services offered are specifically tailored and are sympathetic to each individual or audience. They are designed to demonstrate how to heal, thrive and expand in all areas of life.

Dynamic and passionate, Leonie has a deep joy for seeing people realize their potential. She does this through one-to-one consultations or within a team environment. These treatments and/or consultations can be done via personal appointments or through online media portals.

Leonie has been engaged as a keynote speaker at numerous seminars, conferences, and business events to engage, energize, and empower audiences with her rare blend of knowledge, personality, and motivation.

Leonie's qualifications include certification in the following fields of health and well-being:

- Metaphysics Healing Certification
- Touch for Health Certification
- Diploma in Soft Tissue Manipulation and Massage
- Neuro-Linguistic Programming Practitioner Certification
- EMF Balancing Technique – Advanced Teacher/Practitioner Certification

- Reiki Master Teacher /Practitioner Certification
- Alpha Mind Power Certification
- University of SA - Health Sciences
- Diploma of Herbal Essence Therapy
- Power of Primary Acupressure certification

CHAPTER SIX

KEYS TO HEALING CHILDHOOD PAIN AND TRAUMA

By Leonie Feast-Jones

My passion is assisting people to awaken their potential by connecting with their inner wisdom. I can see into one's unique electromagnetic field, work through and shift the emotional or trauma blockage (known as pain) created in the body's energy system.

Throughout life everybody experiences some level of trauma.

When an individual suffers from a traumatic episode in their childhood years, this can seriously affect their general health and ability to move through life with ease and solve issues that may arise in later years. These may be personal issues, relationship issues, mental issues, or physical, self-confidence, and well-being.

My early childhood trauma was the seedling of inspiration that later became a life-long passion to identify and treat trauma. There were two significant events that would change my life.

1. MY BURNS INJURY

At the age of 5 years, I was standing by an open fire in the lounge room and my nightie caught on fire. From the kitchen, my parents noticed the fire and rushed to the lounge to rip off the burning nightie and wrap me up in a rug. Whilst visiting the doctor, I begged my parents not to take me to the hospital and leave me there. Yet I was dropped at the hospital and sequestered to a large room for three months, separated from my family and my home.

With severe burns to my buttocks, I spent months in hospital lying on my stomach, suffering the painful treatments and multiple skin grafts, feeling completely alone.

For the shy young girl I was at the time, it was a horrific experience to be left in a large hospital room to face this physical trauma by myself, without knowing anyone around me. Having never been away from the family, let alone on my own, this experience set me up for abandonment issues later in life. Being from a farm in a small country town in South Australia and with seven siblings, my parents could only visit me once a week. Part of my recovery was having to learn to walk again. I couldn't walk in a straight line. When I was finally released to go home, along the way my father drove past a large fire at our local timber mill. I was flooded with terror as it reminded me of the flames leaping up in the air from my nightie.

This terrible incident resulted in the harboring of trauma and raw emotions being trapped in my body's electromagnetic field. Later in life I learned a technique to calibrate the past trauma stuck in the back fibers of my body & bring it into my core energy. This allowed me to move the energy through my electromagnetic field, releasing it into my possible future potentials.

I have found this to be one of the most important techniques to use for releasing trauma out of the body's energy fields.

2. FATHER'S TRAGIC ACCIDENT

At the age of 7, my idea of a safe and secure family life was turned upside down, never to be experienced again as it was.

My Dad, a handsome, intelligent, hardworking, and community-spirited person was the only son of a wealthy landholder. He was 32 and working in the logging industry when the unthinkable happened. A large dead limb of a pine tree fell on his head resulting in severe brain damage and a devastating diagnosis regarding his ability to ever work or function effectively as a father or husband again. After several near-death experiences, Dad never returned home and was eventually admitted to a rehabilitation center for the rest of his life. Dad's extremely strong will-power and the willingness to live was said to be a miracle. He survived his accident by a further 32 years.

This life-changing event meant a tragic future for Mum as she was left to raise her large family of Eight children in 10 years alone without the love and support of Dad. The loss of income created serious financial difficulties.

Adding to the woes, the insurance company rejected the claim for compensation due to 'an act of God' clause.

Being children, my siblings and I were never informed about what had happened to our father and the resulting circumstances. This twist of fate seemed like a nightmare. We were farmed out from being together in our safe, secure, loving family environment into different houses and families which felt cold, calculated, and insecure.

This intensified my feelings of abandonment which, as mentioned, showed up in my adult life.

I believe my burns injury and Dad's accident was my ticket to independence and resilience. They became my driver for wanting to succeed in Life Experiences.

Acknowledging and understanding my childhood traumas, Dad's brain injury led me to immerse myself in the study of the mind, brain, and body. I consumed myself into the Natural Therapies industry, studied every modality possible, and fiercely pursued those that resonated with me on every level of my thoughts, beliefs, and value system.

Alpha Dynamics, a powerful Mind power control technique, was learnt by spending many weekends in a live in lock down situation. The weekend live-in workshops were extremely demanding and sometimes fearful teachings. Mastering this modality provided me with the strong foundations for working as a body intuit.

I found a great passion for the study of EMF Balancing Technique. The EMF Balancing Technique is designed to teach you to manage your personal energy, creating a sense of greater stability and balance.

The study of EMF Balancing Technique was undertaken in Australia and then to Sedona in the USA. It taught me Self enablement through the body's electromagnetic field from Head to Heart.

The fundamental theory is: "In the energy of love."

It is a breakthrough modality merging Science and Spirit.

I introduced EMF into Singapore with my teacher, and it has given me a great deal of pleasure to teach the EMF Balancing technique within Australia.

- Anchored by my personal experience and commitment to transformation, I have worked with thousands of people over the years to inspire their healing journey. The foundation of my work is teaching people about energy and the deep connection between mind, body, and experience. Our body holds the energy of experience in its cells – if the predominant experience is joy, we will feel more ease with life; if there has been trauma, this imprint will stay in our energetic field and show up in some way as pain or discomfort until we do the healing work.

This is how I developed "*FEAST ON LIFE FOR LIFE.*"

By CREATING A MINDSET FOR CHANGE TO FEAST ON LIFE FOR LIFE.

Every person has the same capacity as me to turn their trauma into their transformation. They just need to take the time out and learn the process.

To Awaken the Magic Within:

- Tell life how it is for you only.
- Experience your reality with the understanding and knowing that all people have a different reality from yours. Neither person's truth is right or wrong, it's just different.
- Keep doing personal development on yourself till you get it- it's an ongoing process.
- Engage in everything with a loving, kind, open heart.

Observations from my learning are:

- Observe and live in the intuitive side of life.
- Look at all sides and take special notice of the underlying factors - the big picture vantage point.
- Live each day in the Now and practice spontaneity as much as possible.
- Activate life force energy in the body to tap into creative potential.
- To be able to diffuse the darkness (blockages) and experience lasting changes and healing in our lives is essential for optimum wellness.
- Own your own self–patterns, and habits. (see my page for alt)
- What you receive from conception, birth, and the first seven years especially needs to be processed and doing this may be scary and uncomfortable. Without doing this inner work, emotional pain from the past continually influences present day lives.
- Our ability to connect with Passion and purpose is energizing.
- As we express who we are truly, we connect with our emotions.

There is research to suggest most successful people have at some point in their lives:

- Experienced a financial crisis.
- Had self-doubt.
- Wanted to give up.
- Experienced loneliness and isolation.
- Focused on the result, not the process.
- Been driven by their passion, enthusiasm, and strong belief in what they are doing.
- Never accept defeat no matter what!
- A vision and strategic plan.

Once I understood the pain and trauma from my childhood, I developed the ROW Principle to cope.

Imagining you are in a boat and using the ROW Principle.

ROW PRINCIPLE

Yes, time eventually heals wounds, but it doesn't shift the inner trauma. On the contrary, it buries it deeper. Thus, trauma is best to be dealt with because it's locked in the cellular memory.

Your energy system could define who you are, how you heal and how quickly you move on from trauma, challenges, and setbacks. It's not the life challenges themselves, but rather how quickly you can acknowledge the part you played in it and move on

They key is to access the memory and then learn how to release the pain from your body fields. Become an empowered adult engaged in the flow of life by implementing this principle:

RECOGNIZE where you are in life (your boat).

OWN it.

Be **WILLING** to change and **move** on in the **now**.

Recognize:

- Start to observe the habits and patterns of your life.
- What holds you back from feasting on life?
- Which fork in the river of life are you going to choose?

Own the part you play:

- Blaming, hating, punishing, controlling, and rescuing will keep you stuck.
- Take responsibility by acknowledging and understanding your part in the experience.
- The process of owning cultivates awareness.
- Until you own it you will keep repeating the same experience.

Willingness to change:

- Change only comes from the inside and this commitment will help to relieve the pain.
- Wanting to change must be recognized. Ask yourself:
  - What am I willing to change?
  - Am I going with the flow or swimming against the tide?
  - Am I treading in lower vibration energy (blame, hate, punishing, etc)?
- It's not a race! You may need to meander. Take your time in the here and now to process what has surfaced.
- Enjoy change. Every day reveals new and exciting challenges.

Freedom comes when we realize the only person we can change is yourself.

Different personalities can respond however they want and that needs to be okay.

Be responsible only for your own emotions and personal perceptions of your truth.

If you are not willing to transform into your unique self, then you may be stuck forever.

My Five Magic secrets to healing childhood Pain & Trauma

Teaching the dynamics of energy and learning why you need to understand yourself energetically and those around you to "Feast on life for life."

Through my Healing work I have worked with so many different personalities. It showed me that your energy system can define who you are, how you heal & how quickly you move on from the trauma, challenges, and setbacks.

It is not what challenges you have in life; it's how quickly you can acknowledge the part you played in it and how quickly you move on from the trauma.

1. Embrace being Willing to Change:

Enjoying change – every day is a new and exciting challenge!

These are opportunities to rediscover who you are in each moment.

I'm sure we can agree most people find change difficult. In my personal experience, the choices I made required me to learn to embrace change. It took bravery to leave the safe environment of a small country town mentality to move into a city environment to further my learning. As a result, I now like to take the time to make the most of every situation.

I allowed transforming threat into challenge and, through the healing techniques I studied, am well equipped in guiding you through change and assisting in the embracement of new ideas and direction.

21-day Affirmation:

I Am willing to Change!

I Am willing to change my mind!

I Am willing to change my Heart!

I Am willing to change the perception of myself and the world around me!

I Am willing to change what I do and how I do it!

I Am willing to know change, to be changed, and see the miraculous change that change brings!

I Am willing to be transformed, to have my true mind restored, according to Spirit's perfect plan.

2. The dynamics of the Energy system.

Tapping into your energy field – sustaining your energy.

Tapping into your dynamic self by looking at your electromagnetic field and seeing the blockages that hold you back from peak performance.

To be on the cutting edge you need boundless energy. This is achieved by letting go of the old trauma in the back-long information fibers, calibrating it into the core energy to allow it to move into the possible future potentials.

Energy is linked up with the whole of the body and you can feel and sense it all through the Body systems.

Energy becomes power through conscious use.

It's important to connect with your energy system and get your chi going, especially if you are feeling flat and lifeless.

Working to find the power of your intention each year for Focus & Self Discovery. Once you create a roadmap for achieving the intentions, you can then choose to empower yourself.

This gives you greater clarity & effectiveness by weaving the essence of the statement of focused intent into the synchronicities and the realities of your daily lives.

It can give you direct access to your Inner wisdom.

Look at your personal experience in life that will help to achieve your power of intention.

Work with the experiences of strengths and look at the experiences of your challenges in life; know that all experiences can be seen as energy. Not good or bad energy, simply energy or energy patterns that can be managed. Nothing is wasted in your history, and every experience can eventually be turned into a gleaming, golden column of wisdom and support.

Your thoughts, words, actions, and emotions generate energy charges.

We then become more mindful of how we spend our energy in everyday life.

I look at every situation, negative and positive, and find the diamond in it.

"Always look for the Diamond in everything."

3. The energy pattern of self-enablement through the chakra system

Understanding the energy pattern of self-enablement is an important facet in our evolution.

Radiating from the chakras are fibers of light & energy. These fibers form figure eight loops that feed into long vertical fibers of energy that surround & permeate our energy anatomy. Just as the physical anatomy has many systems within it, so does the energy anatomy.

Working within the energy fields teaches how to become Self Enabling-through

- Self-healing,
- Self-learning,
- Self-supporting,
- Self-direction,
- Self-attitudinal thinking,
- Trusting the Intuition

Back yourself – "there is nothing I cannot achieve."

Work with techniques for letting go of past setbacks, family traits, and building empowerment through acknowledging the common thread that prevents you from moving forward.

Health and wellness – sustaining an abundance of energy, vitality, and Passion for life ignites your hunger for fulfillment and introduces powerful life techniques to nourish, nurture and engage your body, mind, and soul.

When you feel anxiety arising and feel stressed then do something different to shift your energy:

Brain gym.

Step back and ask yourself what do I need to change?

Go for a walk.

Do something different.

4. Learning to let go of Panic & anxiety to find Passion & purpose:

People with anxiety disorders are often prone to frequent worrying, feelings of nervousness, and negative thinking. Many people with panic disorder spend time worrying about the future or stressing about the past. Fortunately, relaxation techniques can help counteract these symptoms. Meditation is one of the relaxation activities that aims at assisting you in slowing down your thoughts, letting go of stress, and going into a deep relaxation. This technique can help counteract many of the cognitive and physical symptoms of panic, disorder, and anxiety.

PRACTICE GRATITUDE - Waking up every day having some gratitude thoughts for the day, even the smallest of things, may help relieve stress and anxiety by focusing your thoughts on what's positive in your life.

Spending a moment in gratitude will shift your energy & enable you to think about how you can pay this experience forward.

Throughout this journey I came to understand how passionate I was in the healing world and making a difference in people's lives by working with a variety of healing modalities. I studied many techniques through my journey and, in my practice, utilized the ones that resonate most.

Awareness of self.

Ask yourself "What within myself do I love?"

Personality profiling and numerology helps in understanding what, why, when, who, and the "how" of yourself to find purpose in life.

I learnt this is truly a gift in life to be able to share my skills and knowledge in my healing abilities through the understanding of Body, Mind & Soul.

By being a part of my patient's healing journeys and seeing the outcomes they were experiencing, I was awakened to my own purpose and love.

I learnt, "you can't know till you know."

5. Meditation/Mindfulness

I meditate regularly to stay focused as it is the most powerful tool for creative energy and empowerment. By doing this practice every day I learnt to go within and heal my Body, Mind & Soul for Peace, becoming mindful in everything I do.

By practicing Meditation, it took me back into the Alpha state and our Brain Rhythms.

Alpha Rhythms (Sub Conscious) 14 rhythms per sec.

We are born in a state of Alpha Brain Rhythms.

A spiritual world is our most creative level of rapid healing, high energy, enhanced memory concentration, intuitive knowing, and learning.

This stays with us through ages 1 – 7 years (approx.)

Create your own story.

Beta Rhythms (Outer Conscious) 21 rhythms per sec.

After the age of 7 years, we began to operate in Beta Brainwaves, associated with logical analysis, reasoning thinking, planning, and systematic organization.

It is also a level of worries, fears, doubts, skepticism, sarcasm, stress, tension, and fatigue.

Negative thinking is common at this level.

Ability to master the state of stillness is powerful - having the awareness of having positive thoughts and creating healing from not doing all the time.

"Need to be, not to do."

Whilst feeling depressed and anxious try to create some laughter or watch a funny movie.

Learn relaxation & stress control – "out of the head and into the heart."

To eliminate the daily stresses, we need to perform subtle techniques to assist in switching off from the head and dropping into the Heart from within, and in turn, enhancing focus and direction to move forward.

Creative visualization and achieving excellence – create, see, and experience techniques for focusing the mind to enhance your true creative alpha state for clear, concise, and creative vision and direction for your life.

Make sure your energy is at optimum level by fueling the body with the best food it can have.

Give your temple (the body) exercise and a laughing lifestyle.

Then you need to do a Reflection each year with gratitude on how far you have progressed in life.

And last, of all, for me, I love the travel and lifestyle that has come with the sharing, caring and new learning in each new adventure, no matter what.

Watch your thoughts. Your thoughts are powerful because that is what you become.

Meditation helps drop into a state of calm and peace.

Work with Simple and accessible tools.

If you never take the step to do the work on yourself, then you are always going to be in the "washing machine on recycle."

Case study:

An 18-year-old female suffered panic & anxiety attacks for the last 5 years.

She suffered her first anxiety attack at the age of 7 when her parents divorced.

At this young age she did not understand what was happening and the attacks re-occurred at the age of 18. Not only did the attacks scare her, but she also found it difficult to go out in public and became housebound.

By working within her energy system to realize the blockages in her fields caused by the stress of the anxiety, her life force energy in her physical body was activated and her creative potential ignited.

To be able to diffuse the darkness (blockages) and experience lasting changes and healing in her life was essential for her optimum wellness and healing.

I worked with her to relax her into a meditative state. This allowed her to release the stress and tension in her fields. I also offered breathing techniques to work with when she felt an attack coming on. Knowing that panic attacks may still occur, she was now able to deal with them more effectively as she was learning various techniques, including breathing methods.

She responded well to the treatment and techniques and has been able to venture outside in public again.

Case study:

A 27-year-old male came to me after suddenly developing Bell's palsy which manifested quite quickly on one side of the face. This is the paralysis of the seventh cranial nerve which supplies the muscles of the face. The paralysis caused a characteristic grimace involving the mouth, eye, and forehead, and became swollen and sore. This scared him and his family.

In his first session I worked in his energy field and found trauma in his body fields that stemmed from birth. He was born with club feet which led him to four operations before the age of 4. Later, he had several motor-bike accidents and sustained a hit on the head. This created blockages in his meridians through his body. Over time, through excessive stress his body's nervous system shut down.

Realizing the trauma from the back history and calibrating it into the core energy allowed the energy through his system to flow. This treatment, coordinated with many other methods, allowed him to feel relief and improvement of the nervous system.

Over time the body was allowed to heal.

Please visit the link below:

Free meditation: https://feastonlife.com.au/meditation-breakthrough/

Rika MANSINGH

Bestselling Author/ Registered Dietitian (Clinical, Consultant, Media)/Certified Meditation & NLP Master Practitioner/ Philanthropist & Podcaster

www.rikadiet4wellness.com

info@rikadiet4wellness.com

Rika Mansingh, RD, B.Sc. Dietetics(UNP), PG.Dip.Diet(UKZN), DCEP(CA), is a Registered Dietitian (Clinical, Consultant, Media) in Canada, Bestselling Author of the book, "The Empowered Mind Diet Equation –Get To The Best Version Of Yourself Via Diet & Mind," Certified Meditation & NLP Master Practitioner, Philanthropist and Podcaster.

She received her Bachelor of Science in Dietetics Degree (2002) and Postgraduate Diploma in Dietetics (2003) at the University of Natal in South Africa. Rika moved to Canada in 2008, completed further studies in Dietetics (DCEP), obtained her full registration with the College of Dietitians of British Columbia, and is a proud member of Dietitians of Canada.

Rika is currently working as a consultant dietitian in private practice, a clinical dietitian in long-term care, and a media dietitian, engaged in public speaking events such as the Gluten-free Expo -Canada's largest Gluten-free event. Rika has over 21 years of experience in the dietetic profession and has written articles for newspapers and magazines and broadcast on radio and TV shows in Canada and South Africa. Rika firmly believes that the mind is our most powerful asset, and the brain can change through neuroplasticity.

Rika is extremely passionate about Neuro-linguistic Programming and is committed to supporting, educating, and empowering clients to reach their highest potential and achieve their goals for improved overall health.

CHAPTER SEVEN

YOU ARE THE GAME CHANGER: EVERYTHING YOU WANT IS ON THE OTHER SIDE OF CHANGE

by Rika Mansingh

"We are the ones we've been waiting for. We are the change that we seek."
— Barack Obama.

If you picked up this book, I take it you have been on your own challenging journey and it has brought you to this point. You're seeking something MORE! Congratulations on getting here! You are NOW in perfect alignment with the universe, and everything you have experienced and survived up until this point has led you to this present moment and these powerful words. You are not reading this chapter by mere chance or coincidence. It's all ideal timing, magically synchronized to EMPOWER YOU to TRULY AWAKEN the magic within. I warmly invite you to fully immerse yourself into this chapter and inhale this BREAKTHROUGH moment. You're ALREADY many steps deeper and closer to leading a happier, more fulfilled life, and I am SO excited to embark on this journey with you. Whether you're holding the soft cover, scrolling through your Ebook, or hearing the audio - Keep reading, keep listening, and stay on this path!

No matter where you have been or what setbacks you may have faced, today you get to begin again. Realize and affirm that you are worth it, whole, complete, enough on your own, and deserve the world of opportunities, breakthroughs, and unlimited abundance that's emerging right now. HAPPINESS, PEACE, JOY & FULFILLMENT are yours to claim. The magic is in YOUR hands and YOUR MIND. The most crucial, key ingredient to embrace is CHANGE! The DECISION to CHANGE IS POWERFUL beyond measure!

Earlier on in my journey and while growing up, I heard the saying, "Life is like a roller coaster ride." I knew there would be ups and downs, with good days and bad days, and I knew that when there were bad days, "this too shall pass," and it wouldn't be long before I picked up again, as long as I stayed on the track. My roller coaster ride during childhood and into adulthood was magnificent. I had been blessed to grow up in a wonderful, loving family, my pillar of strength, an inspiring dad, my strong and caring mum, my creative brother, and an energetic extended family who created a lively atmosphere with fantastic music and dance moves galore. While in South Africa, I enjoyed working as a clinical and consultant dietitian in private practice and did media work for the newspaper, radio, and satellite TV. My roller coaster had soaring heights and breathtaking precious moments, which I am grateful for today. After getting married, I moved to Canada. So young, excited, and enthusiastic to move to a country I had never visited before. Experiencing snow for the very first time was beautiful. Learning how to drive on the other side of the road was an exciting challenge. Day by day, I was amazed at the warm, friendliness of Canadian people despite the cold weather.

I continued on my journey as life continued, and then suddenly, I found myself viciously jolted on my roller coaster track. So, here I am, sitting in my roller coaster cart, and it is no longer going up into the clear blue sky but instead crashing through a series of downward spirals. I was going through a divorce. For those of you who have been through a divorce or any difficult situation or similar circumstance, you would agree when I say it is definitely not easy. There were challenging emotions day by day, and I had to learn how to master them and control them before they controlled me. The key is to stay on track. While on my roller coaster, I once met a girl in a restaurant who had an interesting tattoo on her hand. I am curious, by nature, about people and their journeys, and I seek every opportunity to learn from them. I curiously asked this girl, "What made you get a bow and arrow tattoo?" Her reply was something I will never forget, a response that made a massive impact on my mind and how I moved forward afterward, by literally moving backward. She said, "The bow and arrow — sometimes we have to take a few steps back before we can move full steam ahead." A simple conversation shot an arrow into my mind and directed it to focus on being grateful. Our setbacks make us stronger; they are blessings in disguise. Finding the positives in every situation, seeing that silver lining, and being grateful, make one thankful, optimistic, and resilient. I had realized that no matter what circumstances the universe sends our way — the way we handle it — boils down to two words - OUR CHOICE, and it's not just one choice, we have MANY choices. We decide how we allow situations to affect us. We give the situation the power to control us, or we take control and become empowered by it. I chose the latter.

I had made a DECISION to be strong and independent in Canada while my family was back in South Africa. After all the studying I had completed to be here, I wanted to continue to follow my passion and become a successful dietitian in Canada. I had a gut feeling that my purpose in life was to help people through food and nutrition, and I was determined to inspire, motivate and empower people to get to their highest, happiest potential no matter what they have been through or what setbacks they have faced. It has been my calling and true purpose, fueling me with the innate drive daily, to make a difference and CHANGE lives. I have been a registered dietitian for over 21 years and am immensely grateful that my bestselling book, "The Empowered Mind Diet Equation -Get To The Best Version Of Yourself Via Diet & Mind," and podcast, EMDEQ Power, have reached and helped thousands of people from around the world, transform to the best version of themselves. Interviewing special, motivational guests, demonstrating how CHANGE and rapid transformation are possible, deeply inspire me, and facilitating change in others to impact lives for the better, brings me tremendous joy and fulfillment. I am incredibly passionate about neuro-linguistic programming and what drew me to use NLP in my practice were its tools it provides, to not only CHANGE habits and behavior but also to SUSTAIN change! According to Psychology Today, NLP is widely known as the "fastest and most powerful vehicle for personal change in existence!" I have seen many patients who eat for emotional reasons or engage in automatic, addictive habits and behaviors, keeping them stuck in unhealthy, self-sabotaging patterns. Patterns that block them from AWAKENING their inner magic. Trigger after trigger, many people remain on autopilot mode, falling prey to the brain's negativity bias, inundated with limited beliefs, generating automatic behaviors, and wiring the brain to remain in those unwanted, vicious cycles. It's so empowering to know that we can change not only our brains through neuroplasticity but also our minds by becoming AWARE of patterns and making a DECISION to CHANGE. I firmly believe that to AWAKEN the magic within, one has to get UNSTUCK, to unlock one's highest potential and get to the happiest, most fulfilled version of oneself.

Are you feeling empowered to awaken YOUR inner magic? The universe is ready to meet you halfway. You're going to be STUNNED about what's waiting for you on the other side of change as soon as you get unstuck, so let's start moving!

I invite you to discover, WHAT DO YOU WANT? What are you passionate about? If you could do anything at all and failure was not an option – What would you do and for what purpose? What's holding you back from living the life of your dreams? What do you need to change in your life, to make you feel joyful and fulfilled? What limiting beliefs, thoughts, habits, or behaviors keep you from unleashing your inner magic?

Let's pause for a moment. Visualize yourself in the future; 3 months, 6 months, or even a year from now. See this ideal version of you in no particular context, having already conquered your obstacles, removed barriers, achieved your goals and in a wonderful, blissful state. You're in ABSOLUTE AWE of yourself, smiling massively because WOW, you did it! Embody this beautiful image of your future self. See it as a big, bright, colorful, panoramic picture. Fully immerse yourself in this experience and "Whatify" yourself by asking 'what' questions galore; What do you see? What do you hear? What do you feel? What did you have to do, and who did you have to become to achieve this excellent state you're in? And my favorite question that transforms any day into a Thanksgiving Day is – What are you grateful for? As you embrace this spectacular experience, having achieved what you wanted, filled with warmth, brightly colored feelings, and magical sounds, take a moment to realize that everything that led you to this desired state involved YOU making changes. YOU changed from within. There's a beautiful, inspiring quote, "If an egg is broken by an outside force, life ends. If broken by an inside force, life begins. Great things always begin from the inside."

It's true. Real change comes from within when you are WILLING to try something different to create the results you want. YOU are your very own GAME CHANGER. You had to get UNSTUCK, chop and make changes, ride the confusion wave and all other emotional waves, with persistence and tenacity to reorganize your life to live by design, not default. You had to focus on what you WANT and NOT on what you DON'T WANT.

Heraclitus said, "The only thing that is constant is change." So true. Change is constant and something to be embraced. Stagnation is our worst enemy. Here are some booster points to AWAKEN the magic within:

☐ Change Your Beliefs

Our beliefs about ourselves are extremely valuable for grounding transformation. Barriers to change are imaginary. We actually create our own limitations. To make a breakthrough -break free! Break out of the addictive comfort zone. Be open to possibilities and believe in numerous choices. When you feel down and deflated, inhale deeply to the thought of how far you have come. Reflect on past accomplishments and believe in yourself to achieve those desired states again. Delve deep and decide what you want and what you truly value, and engage in behavior that aligns with those values. Your beliefs are paramount and create self-fulfilling prophecies. If you believe you're unfit and unhealthy, you will easily adopt habits to fit this description. AWARENESS is a superpower. When we are aware of a belief, we can change it by repetitively changing our perspectives. Upgrade your beliefs and challenge your ideas about yourself. Choose empowering beliefs. Decide what your belief system is going to be and don't settle for anything less. What you practice will eventually grow stronger and enhance your belief system even more. Every day is a new beginning and an opportunity to choose better, be better and do better. Have faith — it doesn't matter whether you believe in a higher power or not, but most importantly, have faith and belief in YOURSELF.

☐ Change Your Thoughts

The mind can be our biggest barrier to change or the best catalyst to bring about change, depending on how we wire it. When we sprout a negative thought, we should step back, challenge and question these thoughts. Just because we think negative thoughts almost automatically doesn't always mean they are true. Many thoughts are assumptions, interpretations, and conclusions – not the absolute truth. The next time you're on the verge of collapsing into a negative thought pattern, try asking yourself, is this thought really true? What if I am wrong here? How does believing this thought make me feel? Is it a fact or something streaming through from the subconscious mind as an altered perception? Realistic thoughts are positive thoughts when they push you to achieve your goals. Continuous negative self-talk distracts, creates anxiety, and prevents us from achieving our goals or desired joyful states. The route of all negativity is fear. Whether it is fear of loss, fear of getting hurt, worrying about the future—you name it—fear is the culprit. Did you know that 90 % of the things we worry about don't actually happen? William James said, "The greatest weapon against stress is our ability to choose one thought over another." Worrying incessantly and constantly ruminating about the negative is just wasted energy. MANY of our negative thoughts are irrational and affect our emotions. They are termed cognitive distortions. Dr. Mike Dow, a well-known psychotherapist and brain health expert, categorized them as seven pitfall thought patterns: personalization, pervasiveness, pessimism, polarization, permanence, psychic and paralysis analysis. By being aware of these thought patterns, we can change them and reshape our model of reality. Here are some tips to stop giving energy to negative thoughts:

- If something you perceive as negative happens, for example, after sending a long text to a friend, you get a blunt text in return. Don't go off on a tangent thinking, "My text was probably silly. I'm never good at communicating." Watch those thoughts (WTT)! Don't take things personally or blame yourself. Chances are your friend had a busy day, is tired, or is in a rush. Depersonalization feels lighter and allows us to empathize with people, bringing about positive feelings of compassion — a better, more refreshing route.

- If a small part of your day doesn't go according to plan, don't let it filter through to hinder the rest of your day. For example, after a late night and you're in a low mood the next morning, you may say, "Oh no, this day is going to be terrible. I might as well sleep all day." Watch those thoughts (WTT)! Don't give in to hopelessness and helplessness. RISE and choose to turn your day around. Do some stretching exercises, listen to calming music, or guided meditations. Be aware of these activities' uplifting feelings, and remember THIS association the next time you're feeling low and need to bounce back. As the day progresses, things can change. Conquer pervasiveness.

- Avoid catastrophic thinking. Believing the worst about everything and creating scenarios in your mind, about events that may never occur, will drain you. For example, "I didn't eat healthily today, so I'm going to become obese. I might as well give up." Again, question and challenge the validity of your thoughts. Is this true, and do you feel empowered? No. So, watch those thoughts (WTT)! How about saying, "I didn't eat healthily today and that's ok. I will strive to eat healthily from tomorrow as I visualize myself having a healthier mind and body." Your new thinking and new feelings will change your behavior the next new day.

- Living life in terms of absolutes—yes or no, seeing everything rigid, in black or white, is an example of all-or-nothing thinking. We can avoid difficult emotions and stress-inducing mindsets by being more accepting, tolerant, and accommodating. Depolarize yourself. Allow for flexibility in your thinking and you will experience life as a rainbow of bright colors. Did you know that perfectionism is also a way of polarized thinking? Perfectionism can prevent you from being content in the moment while always striving to make things 100 % perfect.

- Nothing is set in stone. Avoid making engraving remarks to yourself, like, "I have always and will always binge eat when I'm upset." Nothing is permanent. Feelings change. View challenging times as temporary. It will pass.

- Don't make assumptions. Acting on beliefs that aren't true can leave you feeling jolted and disappointed. "He didn't call. I think he found our previous conversation dull." Do we know for a fact that this is true? No. So, Watch those thoughts! (WTT)! Mind reading and making assumptions can be unnecessarily harmful.

- A series of negative, irrational thoughts can paralyze you if you get stuck in its negative loop. Surrender is the pathway to letting go. Over-analysis can steer you on a path to emotional paralysis. We are our worst critics and can sabotage ourselves with self-defeating monologues. Don't be so hard on yourself. When you have love and compassion for yourself, you take care of yourself first and share the best version of yourself with others.

The bottom line - don't be a prisoner of your thoughts or other people's thoughts of you. Author and psychiatrist Dr. Daniel Amen mentions in his book the 18:40:60 rule: When you are 18, you worry about what everyone thinks of you. When you are 40, you don't give a damn about what anybody thinks of you; when you're 60, you realize that nobody has been thinking of you at all. People spend their days thinking about themselves, not you. Choose your thoughts wisely.

☐ Change Your Habits

✔ Catch Those Tricky Triggers

We are all human, and as we navigate through our journey of life, we WILL get triggered and sometimes get caught up in a worry spiral, eat emotionally or engage in other unhealthy habits. It doesn't have to be this way. You can break unhealthy cycles. Journal about what triggers you- What do you see, hear, think, and feel just before the triggered habit occurs? You will notice it's usually the SAME negative thoughts, the SAME feelings, and the SAME unhealthy behaviors which follow. Emotions are just chemical responses to a thought and generally last about 90 seconds. We are triggered by something we see or hear, and there's a narration in our minds -a story we tell ourselves. These thoughts give rise to feelings of discomfort, which intensify. It then slowly diffuses and subsides if we are mindful to take a few deep breaths, focus on what we want and switch to gratitude for what we already have. Did you know that the brain can't think of a negative thought when in a state of gratitude? Allow the 90-second wave of emotion to run its course. Bad feelings don't stay bad feelings. Be present with these feelings and watch them evolve. Get creative and think of five healthier habits to replace the habits blocking you from awakening your inner magic. When we engage in healthy habits and feel positive afterward, our brain's neurochemical dopamine is released, and the pleasure reward system is activated. We can replace old neural pathways with new ones and with repetition, positively rewire our brains. Did you know that the dopamine reward response from healthy activities is much stronger than the dopamine response, producing pleasure from unhealthy activities? This is empowering, for sure!

When triggered, you're likely over remembering the past or over-thinking the future, taking away from the present moment. There's a quick neuroscience-backed hack to bring you to the present moment. It's the 5-4-3-2-1 Grounding Technique, where you take a deep breath and count down from 5. At 5, bring your attention to 5 things you can see. At 4, acknowledge 4 things you can touch, then 3 things you can hear, 2 things you can smell, and lastly, 1 thing you can taste. Take a deep breath and re-evaluate how you feel. This technique can help you build rapport with yourself, break automatic patterns, and make you feel more powerful than your situation.

✔ Push Past Procrastination

Great ideas are wonderful building blocks when setting goals to achieve your dreams, but excellent EXECUTION is key to get you to where you want to be! When you accomplish a task, your brain starts to think, "If I did that, imagine what else I can do," and BOOM, suddenly, the world seems full of possibilities. Procrastination will NOT give you your desired results, and it's just a mindset that can be changed with awareness, effort, and commitment. When we are clear about what we want and for what purpose, MOTIVA-TION happens automatically, and we keep going strong, with good momentum.

✔ Flip, Flop, Chop, and Change Perspective.

Take TIME to become a WATCHER: With each tick-tock of the clock, pause, breathe, and become the observer, witnessing for a few moments any difficult situation you're dealing with from a different view. Step back, pull out, and float away– aerial, horizontal, or diagonal. Separate yourself. See the situation from your position, then flip-flop to put yourself in the 2nd person's position (try adding some empathy and compassion here). See the situation from the viewpoint of a 3rd person just observing. You can also choose your own adventure by assuming the mental viewpoint of a coach, doctor, Oprah, or even Papa Smurf. Re-examining the situation from different positions reduces the stimulus, so you're not overly associated and overwhelmed, and this will help you see things in a completely different light.

✔ Intensify Your Intentions

Set an intention at the start of each day by visualizing your day, what you wish to accomplish, and how you want to feel at the end of your day. If you suspect any obstacles, create a master plan to guard against the autopilot processes that derail you by WOOPING up this quick, evidence-based, scientific method called 'mental contrasting with implementation intentions', created by psychology Professor Gabriele Oettingen, after 20 years of studies in human motivation:

- The W in WOOP stands for WISH.

-Ask yourself what you wish for or want to achieve? State this in the positive. Instead of saying, "I never want to eat junk food." Rather, say, "I want to eat healthily for my mind and body."

- The 1st O in WOOP stands for OUTCOME.

-What does your desired outcome look like? Bring out all the rewards and benefits & visualize them in as much detail as possible.

- The 2nd O in WOOP stands for OBSTACLE.

-What obstacles could hinder your progress? It's crucial to think of your desired outcome BEFORE the barrier always, so it drives you, energizes you, and pulls you forward towards it. If you visualize the obstacle before the outcome, WOOP would get WARPED, and the technique won't work.

- The P in WOOP stands for PLAN.

-What would be an effective action thought to overcome your obstacle? Here we install an IF THEN process to overcome the barriers and achieve your goal or the desired state. For example, "If X happens, THEN I will do Y." Give yourself numerous options. We are now prepared for the obstacles and can stay on track by creating "implementation intentions," programming the brain to recognize a pattern and react in a specific, more helpful way.

✔ Prioritize Self-care

Truly decide to take care of yourself, and your life will instantly shift for the better. When our brains are healthy, we are more resilient and happier. Before devouring, we should ask ourselves, "What will this food do for me, and how will it affect how I feel afterward?" As for your social media diet -be mindful of your daily portions, or it may profoundly affect your mental health. Say nice things to yourself, and you will not need validation or affirmation from others to elevate you. Prime your language to weed out words like can't, never, and should. Replace them with can, when and could to keep your focus positive. Do an activity or hobby that will bring you joy and aim to get 7-9 hours of sleep. Schedule meditation in your day and self-monitoring through journaling. Reflection and introspection without distraction will free your mind to explore new ideas and opportunities.

I will end my chapter with Goi Nasu's quote, "Ships don't sink because of the water around them. Ships sink because of the water that gets IN them. So don't let what's happening around you get inside you and weigh you down." The things that happen to you don't define you. Some situations are out of our control, but the way we respond to them, now that's where the power is, and that power comes from WITHIN YOU. A happy, fulfilled life isn't a new place – it's just a new attitude and a CHANGED mindset. The best moments in your life are still on their way. I know how capable you are of transformation, and I BELIEVE in you to AWAKEN your magic within. YOU are the GAME CHANGER & YOU CAN DO IT!

Robert Carbuccia

www.robscoaching.com

https://www.linkedin.com/in/robertcarbuccia/

You may think you know Coach Robert Carbuccia, but chances are, you don't know just how deep his commitment goes.

"I always strive to help people get to a better place through connection and conversation." Says Carbuccia. "It's my goal – My Purpose -- to encourage more Breakthroughs in Life through Transformational Coaching."

Rob Carbuccia has been professionally encouraging others to discover their own hidden talents for more than 25 years. He has a knack for spotting his clients' "special sauce" – and creating a game plan of action for that particular talent - on the spot. Call him an Opportunity Finder. His contribution to hundreds of Real Estate Careers could be calculated in the millions. Millions earned. Facilitating breakthroughs, sometimes painful, is what he does best.

"I am blessed with the ability to really connect with just about anyone and everyone. I feel like I can read people very well." He says. Carbuccia uses the skill set to hone-in on strengths, then through exercises centered around conversational techniques, elicits sometimes emotional reactions leading ultimately to self-discovery. "People tend to open up, the truth comes out, and we can get to the root of negative roadblocks holding them back."

He's much more than a Certified Coach; a dozen years ago, he became a Master Trainer in NLP – Neuro Linguistic Programming. Practitioners are known for applying NLP techniques to achieve work-oriented goals, such as improved productivity or career progression. Matching voice, intonation, and intent – people can be linguistically programmed to elicit certain behaviors. Career seekers who learn the techniques often enjoy serious gains – particularly in sales.

It was after building a successful Real Estate career in New York and Florida that Carbuccia turned his talent to helping others achieve the success he feels so fortunate to have found.

"Many of my clients are in the 40-55 age range, and they are transitioning – much as I did. They are often looking to re-invent themselves. And almost universally, they want life to be different this time around."

Carbuccia facilitates that desire with methods ranging from NLP to Hypnosis and Time Line Therapy, along with study and analysis of DISC – which measures a person's behavioral style. These cutting edge methodologies, married with old school work ethic and tried and true productivity systems, drive success.

"There are many similarities between the two businesses," he says. Referring to both Real Estate and Elite Level Coaching. "In both, I'm helping clients self discover what it is they desire most in life. And often, it's right there in front of them. We figure out the answer to the question, 'What's your purpose? What's your goal'."

"The difference? With Real Estate – we are mostly changing the physical environment. With Coaching – we are changing the psychological/emotional environment."

"What's really cool is that a lot of the Breakthroughs I walk with my clients bring me Breakthroughs in my business as well," Carbuccia says. "When you come from a place of contribution – you'll always find gold."

CHAPTER EIGHT

YOU'RE WORKING WAY TOO HARD!

Five simple lessons that change my life forever.

By Robert Carbuccia

Whether we know it or not, magic has been with us from the beginning. As you'll begin to notice, the challenge we often run into is how do we create an access magic on demand. Is it something that happens by luck or by staring aimlessly into the sky and hoping for something to change? Can we access it as simply as wiggling our nose, like Bewitched? Or do we have a magic wand like Harry Potter that has direct access to magic and how to manifest it when we want and need it is where the true power stands?

Now, many business ventures later and many experiences later, I've taken in, I've taken the time to reflect and pay attention to what that secret press repeated, what was the spark or spell that created those Amazing results in my life, as many of us say time and time again if I knew back then what I know now, you can complete this statement. In this chapter, I will share with you the secrets that I've found to work time and time again when my magic from within was awakened, and I'm certain without a shadow of a doubt that it will be the same for you. These five simple steps will help you gain perspective on your life. See where your strengths really are. Help you focus on what's really most important to you and what will help you set or what will help you get the biggest results.

Step 1
Our Beliefs & Values

Insist on yourself. Never imitate. Every great man is unique.
Ralph Waldo Emerson

What are beliefs? Where did they come from? What are values? Where did they come from? What are your values and beliefs? How do we identify them? Are there good values or bad values? What makes them good or bad? Can we change our beliefs & values after so many years of habitual behavior? If so, then how can we change them? What are your values? What's the most important thing to you about your relationships, career, health, wellness, and spirituality?

Values are what's most important to us.

Beliefs are convictions we trust as being true.

Belief Systems are the structure of our convictions.

Core Beliefs are deep convictions of what is essential.

Understanding that this is a part of our unique makeup as people is the first step in the right direction. According to Sociologist Morris Massey's Developmental Period.

From the ages of 0-7 years old is considered to be the Imprint Period.

Think about what a person is learning during this time. They are simply watching and absorbing all the information that's being put before them.

Whatever it is that they watch on TV, listen to on the radio, learn from a school teacher, the babysitter, the aunt, uncle, mother, father, church, or any religious organization. Children at this age are complete sponges taking in any programming that was already instilled in any of these adults. So unknowingly, at this age, the base operating system is being installed, and we are completely unaware of it. Sure, our parents, depending on how conscious they might be, could control what's being imprinted; however, it's not 100%! So whatever limiting beliefs may come from that adult figure is getting passed down to the next generation. During this time, we accept much of everything that is around us as true. This is a critical period because it's from here that we learn to develop a sense of right and wrong, good and bad. During this time, this blind belief period is where the early formation of trauma is found and other deep problems.

From the ages of 7-14 is the Modeling Period.

During this time, we copy our parents, peers, and people in general. It's like taking a moment to try on a new pair of shoes, a dress, or a new suit. So here you have this archive of new values and beliefs, and it's time to put them to the test. Our teachers and religion are very strong during this time. Many religious organizations refer to this as the pre-teen years. The challenges during this time are more along the lines of hearing, seeing, and noticing contradicting information from everyone around the person. Now it's time to put to the test and create your own values and beliefs based on the results you're getting. The big challenge with this is that if the individual is of a lower SES, social, economic status, then their exposure can be minimal in comparison to other children in this age range. Oftentimes during this time, a teacher or youth leader could have more influence than a parental figure.

From the ages of 14-21 is the Socialization Period.

If you take a moment to look back to this time in your own life, you will notice how during this time is when we as people begin to develop as individuals from the earlier programming. Unconsciously we begin to turn towards people who seem to be more like us. Media such as television and the music we listen to resonates with the beliefs and values of our peers. Think about it, how many teenagers want their parents going with them to see their favorite music group? In some of Dr. Massey's research, he claimed that people are pretty much hardwired once they leave the socialization period, and nothing will change their values and beliefs until and unless they have an emotional experience (SEE - Significant Emotional Event) that provokes them to review, examine and possibly change their initial values and very possible their own beliefs. Remember that our values determine our beliefs. Our values motivate our behavior.

From the ages of 21-35 is the Business & Career Persona Period.

During this time, you begin to model who you relate to in the business arena. Take a moment to think back to who it was that had the biggest influence on you when it came to what you wanted to do or who you wanted to become in your business or career. Many people decide during this period what they are most passionate about and begin choosing or taking courses to develop themselves in this area. Understanding that this is a process that originally stemmed from an early part in our life can make all the difference.

Why, you might ask? Oftentimes we miss the simple rule that the quickest way from one point to another is a straight line. However, it can be very difficult to go in a straight line if you're always navigating through different beliefs and values that stem from others, and you now have to stand firm in what you've noticed to be true. Being true to yourself. Being true to what you're passionate about. Here's a simple exercise to get you started on this path if you haven't taken the time to do this already. Many of our values are connected to the following areas in our life:

- Love
- Wealth
- Relationships
- Health & Wellness
- Spirituality
- Personal Growth

The first thing you want to do is look at the list above and quickly, without any thought to it, choose which ones are the most important to you personally and rewrite them in that new order.

Once you've identified which is the most important one, for example, let's say you chose Personal Growth. Now ask yourself the following question:

"What's important to you in the context of personal growth?"

Now begin to list as many of these items underneath this category as quickly as you can! Let's see how many you can come up with in less than 30 seconds. Set an egg timer or a digital alarm on your electronic device after writing all these items out. Repeat what we first did with the categories. This would be to identify which item is the most important to you and write them down in this order.

Notice what you came up with. Did you notice that what you may have thought was the most important thing to you was not even at the top? Maybe you were already aligned in knowing what was most important to you, and this helped you narrow down your values to where they now have become your minimum standards for your life until something changes in the near future.

Step 2
Perception Is Projection

No problem can be solved from the same level of consciousness that created it.
Albert Einstein

Your beliefs affect your values, and your beliefs and values become the filters through which we view our life and the lives of others; since our perceptions are colored, and are influenced by what we believe to be true, then this dictates how and what we project onto people. One of my favorite examples of this is the story of the man in the New York City Subway who is exhibiting this angry behavior towards everyone. The moment a passenger would get on the train, he would stare into their eyes as if they were responsible for this man's behavior. When he was sitting down, older women would look at him with either fear or disdain because this man would deny the possibility of giving up his seat to anyone. No one dared to look at him with the desire to give up his seat for fear of backlash and a harsh reaction from this crazy man. This was the perception people had of him. So they reacted or projected onto him what they were feeling since the man had his own perceptions.

He, therefore, did the same until someone who boarded the train knew who he was. They saw him in tears and angry. They approached the man by saying, Tom, is that you? The man looked up and saw that it was an old co-worker named Richard. Richard had proceeded to ask Tom, "are you okay?" "How's Susan, Tommy, and Katie doing?" By the time Richard got to the third name. Tom had completely lost it emotionally and broke down into tears. Richard, Tom said, "my family is gone forever. We were on our way to Coney Island for the weekend from Queens, and when. We decided, and we decided to drive because we thought that it would be faster than the train. Unfortunately, we were in a horrible car crash. I was the only survivor in my family."

Notice how this piece of information brings new light into this story. If people on the train had known that this man was grieving the death of his family, would their projections change? Absolutely! So you can see three things at work here. The first perception is a reality to the one doing that perceiving. The second is the more information you have, the more your perception changes. The third is we are each other's projections. I am your projection, and you are mine. One of the Presuppositions of NLP, Convenient Assumptions, is The Law of Requisite Variety: The system/person with the most flexibility of behavior will control the system. So you can see that the magic from within can occur when we take 100% responsibility for our own perceptions and others projections of us. When we do this, instead of dismissing another person's reactions towards us, we can now create the space for curiosity; we can create the space for healing and for providing clarity, which leads me to my next point, communication.

Step 3
Communication Magic

Our words have the power to move hearts, and our hearts have the power to move limbs. Now, that's what I call magic!
Robert Carbuccia

The more I write, the more I'm convinced. Okay, starting over, the more I write, the more convinced I become that every single person that reads these words will come to appreciate the magic of words and how to string them along piece by piece when communicating with others, each more so. Even more so when communicating with self. Since words have power, and our aim is to awaken the magic within them, it becomes obvious that we work on ourselves first so that when we communicate with others, we are using words that open hearts versus words that are closed doors. The biggest challenge that I've seen in my years of Coaching, training, from running Fortune 100 companies or building my own real estate business. When our emotions, combined with our words, become a justification for being authentic. Being authentic or being real, being who you are, is a beautiful thing until it consistently makes others miserable and puts you further away from creating magic and your life. Therefore use what you have learned for good. Use it to edify yourself and the lives of others. In addition to having a tone with conviction behind it just makes this intentional approach with skillful framing versus an emotional outbreak of uncontrolled anger and frustration. This can create a posture of being a victim versus the posture of being an influencer. I want to encourage you to BE the influencer, be the leader, and be the guide. Be the teacher, be the inspiration, and encourage her. After doing this with your communication, notice the reaction people have to you and notice the projections that come back to you. It will be far greater than you could ever imagine.

Step 4
B.D.H..

To be successful, you must be ready to start over. To be successful. You must be willing to do the things today others won't do in order to have the things tomorrow others won't have.
Les Brown

The first time I learned about this distinction in life, I was back in 2010. I was at the point in my life where sheer exhaustion and my daily routine were one in the same. We were one in the same. My real estate business had gone through a boom because of the housing crisis and the amount of homes that went into foreclosure. My life was one big blur. And no matter how much I tried, it seemed as if the needle would never move, week after week, month after month, for several years. Already, the government would change a guideline, and then all those in the real estate industry and all those in the real estate industry had to pivot according to the drop of a dime, or else their deal would not close. A good portion of the real estate agent's income starts. You have to remember that a good portion of the real estate transactions starts with a real estate agent. And commissions are based only and do not owe, and they are commission based only and do not earn a salary and do not get paid. When a transaction doesn't close. The homeowner could always live in their house. If it didn't sell, the buyer could continue to rent. However, the realtor would have invested days, weeks, and months of their time in the transaction and easily not get paid. Because it didn't close. You get the point, and I'll move on from my soapbox and get to the juicy part of this step, B.D.H.

From the day of inception, we are brought into this world and are constantly being taught what to do if we want something. If you want to make more money, then you have to work harder. If you want the home of your dreams, the car you desire, the relationship you've always wanted, then there's something you must do. Notice that it's always a have to or a must and very rarely a "choose to" or "get to" way of thinking. So unconsciously in our lives, we live in a world of constantly doing, day by day. So we can have what we've always wanted. Then we could be happy, joyful, satisfied content, or whatever the word is that you want to add. That's what it would be. Then I learned that this cycle was simply a rat race and needed to change because it was not producing the results that I wanted. Most people don't learn this until they're much older in life. I, however, was fortunate to learn this in my 30's.

Here's the distinction DO, HAVE, AND BE is how we are conditioned to live. So life is always about doing. We continuously chase all the things we've always wanted. Once we have them, you now have the permission to BE. It seems as though there has to be an obstacle course at every turn to achieve that level of peace we've all desired at one point or another in our lives. Then I attended a three-day workshop in New York City. Everything for me changed, and the new trajectory of my life was set in motion, and it literally felt like it rebooted my brain! It's as if a new and updated operating system was installed. Please unplug me from the Matrix or the rat race life. There were several distinctions covered at this workshop, and all were NLP based NLP (Neuro-Linguistic Programming). However, the one that impacted me the most was B.D.H. BE, DO, HAVE! By changing the order of the words, it was like changing the order of the combination to opening a safe with millions of dollars in it. Imagine when baking a pie or a cake, changing some ingredients and the order, the sequence, can create something totally different than what you intended, to begin with. However, when every ingredient is delivered and prepared the correct way, magic happens. This unlocked the hidden potential we've all been carrying around, yet we didn't know how to access it. Since we are human beings, not human doings, it's critical that in all of what is happening in our life, that we stop to take inventory with this distinction.

Ask yourself, where have you been sacrificing your life and energy in pursuit of things that you believe will bring you to the point of peace and calm, enjoy. Instead, choose to be joyful, loving, passionate, ambitious, disciplined, open, driven, responsible, considerate, flexible; you get the picture. Do the activities and watch the results come your way.

Step 5
Energy

Everything is energy. And that's all there is to it. Match the frequency of the reality you want. And you cannot help but get that reality. It can be no other way. This is not philosophy. This is physics.
Albert Einstein.

Up until now, we've looked at the following distinctions:

1. Beliefs and Values
2. Perception is Projection
3. Communication Magic number four
4. BE, DO, HAVE
5. Energy

Energy is the combination of all the distinctions working together in synchronicity; when they come together, you get into the flow of creating magic and awaken the magic within. It's been with you all along, emotional vibration. We are energetic beings, and the sooner we realize that all of our actions and inactions are stitching together the fabric of creation, then the more we will only be operating at our maximum capacity.

Imagine driving a car with four tires, and one of them is flat. No matter how much gas you give it, you will be expending more energy than ever to simply accomplish a 10th of what you would be able to accomplish with the car that had all four tires, full of air at the right measurement. This is what I call, or this is what I mean when I say you're working too hard. Focus on the things you can change. Taking responsibility for your results is the fastest way to awaken the magic within because you and I know we are capable of being extraordinary people.

Robyn Torre

Certified Hypnotherapist / NLP & Mindset Coach / Author

CHAPTER NINE

TRAUMA ENERGETICS

By Robyn Torre

T he process that I use is four techniques that can be used as stand-alone techniques or combined in any combination you wish to use. They are :

1. Moving the Pictures
2. Moving the Emotions
3. Locating the Trauma
4. Hypnosis to Install a Coping Skill

These techniques aren't new, in fact they are decades old but with today's knowledge and energy.

I came across a book entitled Trauma Energetics : A Study Of Held Energy Systems back in 1995 by a gentleman by the name of William Redpath. In it, he describes his journey into trauma with his clients and healing with the use of the submodalities such as VAKOG. For those of you who don't know what this stands for these are the five senses we use everyday and they are:

V Visual

A Auditory

K Kinesthetic
O Olfactory
G Gustatory

He would have his client lay down, face up, on a coach and lightly place his hands either side of their head and ask them questions about these senses with regard to their traumatic experience. Whilst this method can be beneficial to some, it is a very long winded approach but an effective one.

At first glance, I noticed the similarities to NLP but I did not have the knowledge, at that stage, to form an alternate method nor actually understand what was happening both by Mr. Redpath and to his clients.

Back then, NLP was in its infancy and techniques were slowly being introduced and learned by various practitioners, some of which you may know of and learned from yourselves. It wasn't as streamlined as it is today.

I put the book down and pretty much forgot about it until some years later. I had learned about energy healing and the Body/Mind/Spirit connection and how energy interacts with the body to speed up the healing process.

I picked up the book again and reread it. Once I started reading, I couldn't put it down. Suddenly, a whole new world of NLP came to life for me. I started to recognise techniques I had learned over the years that would do the same job and garner the same results as he got by using the body first.

Energy medicine has been introduced. New discoveries about the body were being made. Energy healing was a thing. The techniques were fun and laughter was the new way to reset your Vagus Nerve. Instant self hypnosis, with eyes wide open that anybody could do, was being talked about and taught. Books with scripts were being published and new modalities were being introduced.

But one thing that hasn't changed is the trauma that people suffer. Doesn't matter how it happened, just that it did and now they're suffering because they are unaware of how to heal it. Some people believe that trauma, depression and anxiety can't be cured, so live with it. Well, nothing could be further from the truth.

A mentor in the UK once told me about a client of his that came to him with depression and anxiety. He compelled her to look up under hypnosis and notice the sky, the trees, the clouds, the buildings. It turns out that inducing a State change was a simple and effective pattern interrupt. His comment to me was, could it be that simple? The answer is Yes it can. I have heard of many examples of this type of State change with excellent results. We often look for complex and complicated answers to questions when there is a simple answer. In fact, the simpler the better it turns out. Try it for yourselves and notice what happens.

Another of my mentors is on the spectrum and subsequently wrote a book about hypnosis helping on this spectrum. I asked his opinion about the body/mind/spirit connection and using this, together with energy healing such as spinning energy, as a therapy. His response was that any manipulation of energy however you do it, works down to the epigenetic level and down into the DNA and works on the body for between 4 – 6 months.

This was very heartening because we know that repetition is the key to learning anything. The more you do it, the more it becomes an automatic process. Strengthening the new connection in our subconscious over a 30 day time period is all it takes. So the extra time is a bonus. It meant that I could use it as a post-hypnotic suggestion for the subconscious to deal with other issues that arise from the original trauma as an automatic process. Solve, Resolve, Dissolve.

William Redpath achieved some great results, albeit over many years of therapy. In my experience, people want instant results. However, he did make some interesting observations that gave me pause for thought. One of which was that he suggested that the subconscious has a code or sequence that it must go through before it will offer up trauma for healing. Your subconscious knows what this sequence or code is but it won't give it to you for obvious reasons. Seemingly a catch 22 situation.

It must be satisfied that you have learned a lesson before it will let it go. Another thing he did was to attach colors to various stages of healing. He and his colleagues of the day suggested that the color gold was the most healing color there was.

My use of these techniques has been created because of my observations and learnings and I have achieved the same results as he did but over half an hour rather than over many years. Every person I have used this technique on has finished with the color gold, without any prompting from me at all. I attribute the color gold with their life force and use this to induce trance.

Over the years, I have learned many wonderful techniques in healing, such as NLP, Mindset and Hypnosis. These three combined are the basis of my technique. I think the biggest thing was that body/mind/spirit works best. There were teachers that would help you quiet your conscious mind so that suggestions would make a take in your subconscious. But with body/mind/spirit, if you use the body to do the change work, then the mind will follow with no resistance and if you're having fun, then your conscious mind will not interfere in the process, rather, it will just sit there as an observer while you have fun. When was the last time you were out at lunch or dinner with friends and laughing until you almost fell off your chair, got a bit tipsy, and just enjoyed yourself? Remember that time now. Ask yourself did your conscience interfere with this and say, "am I having fun yet", "is this where I laugh". No, you didn't. The conscious mind was quiet, acting as an observer, just idling. So the key is to have fun. If you want to be happy for no reason, try this method.

I learned this technique from one of my mentors in San Diego. Thank you David. Think about the above example, about being happy and laughing. Notice where in your body you feel it and point to it. Notice also that there is a thread attached to that happy feeling and follow it out in front of you. If you can't see the picture in front of you somewhere, take a guess where that picture might be, first impressions. Most often, you will guess correctly. But, just to make sure, bring that picture out in front of your face. Notice what happens when it gets close to your nose. Now move it back at arm's length from your face and notice how that feels. Make the picture smaller and notice the feelings, put it behind your head and notice how that feels. Bring it back in front of you and write down how it feels for you and keep that with you. Just the words about how it feels. Now make the picture blanket sized and put it over your head so it reaches the ground all around you and notice how that feels. When you've got that, take it off and make it regular size again and put it back into the grid. When you want to feel happy again, bring it out and put it on. Easy. Keep your notes for later.

The language of the subconscious is pictures and emotions. If you have a picture of something with a strong emotion, it will make a connection in your subconscious. Our words have pre-attached emotions and that's why we use those words to describe how we feel, our surroundings, love, hate, everything.

Because the sequence or code to unlocking the trauma isn't known to us, the next best solution is to unpack, if you will, the trauma by removing the pictures, removing the emotions and replacing them with what you would rather be feeling, learning a lesson and then finding and unlocking the trauma. Remember, you cannot change the event itself, but you can change how you feel about it now.

Here's a fun exercise for you to try. Sit in a chair in front of a table or similar surface. Put your arms on the table and your head down into your arms and say negative stuff such as I'm unhappy, I'm lost etc and then tell yourself out loud how good you feel and notice what happens instead. Now sit up straight with a smile on your face, thinking good thoughts and tell yourself out loud how bad you feel and notice what happens instead. Most people start laughing. This is what we call a State change exercise.

I would like you now to approach this next section with an open mind, setting aside all bias and be the smart, intelligent people that you are and able to follow instructions. That's all it takes. Combine this with the thought that everything works. You just haven't found the one that works for you yet. But you will with the last ingredient of having fun.

These are techniques that can work for anyone. In other words they can be used individually or together. They don't require you to believe, they only require you to follow the instructions and use your body to do the change work. By using the body to make the change, the mind will follow with very little to no resistance.

1. Move the Pictures

This brings us to the first of my techniques, moving the pictures. The grid we used to locate the happy pictures is called the proprioceptive grid and holds your open files and currently playing files just like on a computer. Anything behind your head are closed files and archived files. But you can't just take a picture out of the front and put it behind your head without dealing with the attached emotions when trauma is present because your subconscious will not allow you to deal with it unless it is satisfied that you have learned a lesson first.

These pictures of trauma are often really big, right in front of your face, in color and some of the many symptoms are to make you feel sick to your stomach, give you headaches, nightmares, cold sweats, flashbacks. The list goes on and is different for everyone. So, the first thing is to pick a spot on the horizon and put your hands in front of your eyes, palms facing that horizon and give the picture a really hard shove away from your face towards that spot you chose. If it isn't far enough away from you, give it another push really hard until it is a small picture. Then draw a big black frame around the now smaller picture with your fingers so you know how big it is and to contain it so it doesn't get bigger again. Remember the knobs on radios or in your car to control volume, reach out and feel under the bottom edge of that frame until you find a small knob like that and turn it to the left which will black out the picture totally and notice how that feels to you. Then turn the knob back to the center and over to the right and white the picture out totally and notice how that feels to you. Which feels better, the black or the white. Choose which one feels better and turn the knob in that direction and leave it there. Now use your imagination and imagine the pointy fingers on each of your hands is now a biro filled with gold ink. Start writing on the picture with both fingers. Doesn't matter what you write, pictures are OK too, keep writing until you think you have written enough. The picture will scroll with you so you never have to worry about running out of space to write.

Once you've finished writing, lift the picture up and float it back to another horizon way back in the distance and watch it disappear. With your most dominant hand make a fist and bang it into the palm of your other hand and say BANG BANG BANG BANG just like a nail gun. This gives your sub-conscious the message that it has been nailed back there and doesn't require any further attention. Notice how that feels and also notice that the pictures are gone.

2. <u>Move the Emotions</u>

The next step is the moving of the emotions. We don't want to get rid of these emotions because they may be attached to other events that you may want to keep.

This is a very old technique I learned but with the advent of energy healing it was the ideal choice for moving emotions quickly and efficiently. It's called the Swish Technique, where you swish the emotion away and replace it with what you would rather be feeling. Please keep in mind that we are not trying to replace a tragic and traumatic event with happy feelings or a band aide. We cannot change the event but we can change how we feel about it now and this is what we are going to do here. There are many variations of this technique that you may have heard of.

You're going to need a pen and paper for this exercise. The idea is to write down the pain point, giving it a score between 1-10, 1 being the least and 10 being the most, together with what emotions come up for you.

Start by sitting up straight in a chair, eyes facing front, hands in your lap and relaxed. Breathe.

Using your intuition and first impression, look top left and write down the emotion and intensity, same for middle left and then bottom left and top right, middle right and bottom right following the same procedure.

Reach out with your most dominant hand, grab hold of those emotions, wherever they are and swish them to the other side in a throwing motion. On a surface in front of you or into your other hand, use your fist and then say the words BANG BANG BANG like hearing a nail gun, nailing it into place. This gives your subconscious the impression that it doesn't need to worry about trying to keep them over there. Job done.

Now remember those wonderful happy emotions you found in step 1 and find those starting top left, middle left, bottom left and top right, middle right and bottom right, noting the pleasure point between 1-10, 1 being the least, 10 being the most and the emotions that come up for you. Reach out and grab those emotions, wherever they are and swish them into where the unwanted emotions just were. Same process, with your dominant hand and the words BANG BANG BANG, nail them there. Once you take something away, you must put something back or your subconscious will put something in there to fill the hole that might be even worse than what you took out so swish in your emotions of happiness and healing. Notice how you feel now. Has the pain point changed? If it's down to 0 that's great. That's what we're aiming for, but If not, why not.

I remind you that this process is all about you, so what do you think you need to do to make it a 100% success for you. Put it in there, change it and nail it into place the same way as before. I'm teaching you to heal yourselves by asking you questions about how you feel and what you would rather have and feel. Putting you back in control.

Also, the best way to stimulate the vagus nerve is with laughter and happiness, having fun, so having you buzzing with the emotions of happiness and healing and vibrancy, that are induced by your own words and emotions, radiates out from you and are delivered to the rest of the body.

3. <u>Locating the Trauma</u>

The third step in the process is to locate the trauma. The subconscious is now ready to offer up the trauma for healing because the code or sequence has been met. With no pictures and emotions attached to the trauma now, the subconscious is left with just the held energy. It isn't protecting you from anything now so I am willing to give it up.

It will be in a certain place. If you and I were face to face, I would know exactly where the trauma is because you would subconsciously tell me at the beginning of this trauma session. Body language, eye access and the words you used would tell me but mainly the visuals. However, for this exercise, we will assume that the trauma is in the middle chest area, somewhere between the breasts, just near your heart. My clients usually complain of heartburn, stomach ache, headaches and/or nausea. However, once a doctor has ruled out any medical issues, which is the first question I ask on arrival, if they haven't sought medical advice, then they are directed to do so before we can proceed with anything. Once this requirement has been satisfied, the session will now proceed. I ask you to imagine you can see a toggle switch on the right hand side, +bigger and –smaller. This is for safety reasons so that you have a way of controlling the trauma. If the image gets too much for you, simply make it smaller, but not too small so as to not be able to notice details. Please resist the urge to erase the image altogether. This will exacerbate the trauma because it has not been dealt with so it will come back. I then ask you to close your eyes and with your inner eyes, locate the trauma and tell me what color it is, what shape is it, what's the texture, does it have a smell, a taste, what does it feel like, can they move it around like up and down, move it from inside to outside.

Very often, anyone with trauma feels out of control because they can't control what's happening to them. This step is to give them back the feeling of control and change their focus away from the past and what their trauma did and is doing to them. By now they're feeling better and more in control because the fear is gone. The subconscious is now giving up the trauma for healing.

I ask you to reach out and touch the black object. Turn it around in your fingers, what's it doing and are there any cracks on it. What colors, if any, are coming out of it. It's important to keep asking questions about the object and keeping tabs on how you are feeling.

Once you have located that crack, I ask you to make the image bigger so that you can see into it and make it even bigger so that you can step into it easily. Keeping constant communication with you and asking questions like what color is the light, can you access it, what do you think you need to do with it.

At this is the point the black shell usually cracks and falls away and the trauma has been offered up for healing. The color is usually gold and that's because it is your life force. The held energy is now released and all the symptoms are gone or fading and energy is flowing freely again.

4. Hypnosis to Install a Coping Skill

Reveling in this euphoric feeling of freedom, relaxation and peace, this last step in the process flows naturally which is a light hypnotic trance to install a coping skill and post hypnotic suggestions for the future.

If you are not aware, all hypnosis is self hypnosis and you are always in total control of the process. It is usually part of the process and agreed with you before trance is induced that if you're not sure you like what you're hearing then you will come out of trance, open your eyes and say so. We can talk about it and then go back into trance again if you wish to. I have not included a hypnotic script here because it will be different for each person.

You can use these techniques for any change you wish to make, not just for trauma. Remember the key is to have fun, use your imagination, laugh lots.

I hope you enjoy these techniques as much as I have over the years.

Sharmini Ratnasingam

Certified NLP coach / Empowerment Coach / Author / Artist / Professional Musician / Experienced Corporate Professional.

https://sharmqwest.com

Sharm was born and raised in Malaysia and is a certified NLP coach, empowerment coach, author, artist, professional musician and experienced corporate professional.

She was constantly immersed in the arts and attributed her creative side to her mother, and her father's beliefs tempered her personality in life and its existence. Although disciplined and strict, her parents' nature and upbringing set her on the path to expressing her point of view openly and confidently.

She started her career with Malaysia Airlines as a musician, an interest that stemmed from her school days. She was a professional trombonist (the first female trombonist in Malaysia) in several local orchestras.

Her two worlds were closely intertwined, with two completely different mindsets and disciplines. Music influenced her work, and her work influenced how she approached her music. She felt privileged to be able to move in both worlds, which allowed her flexibility in her understanding and approach.

After more than 33 years with the airline, she finally ventured into the next phase of her life. She is curious about nature and loves to explore and experiment. 2022 was her year of discoveries and unique opportunities that took her out of her comfort zone. As a coach, she is inspired to remind people of their own values and the importance of living the life we are each given.

CHAPTER TEN

REINVENTING YOUR LIFE - FIVE LESSONS IN EMBRACING CHANGE TO REACH YOUR TRUE POTENTIAL

By Sharmini Ratnasingam

My experiences, both good and bad, have helped shape the person I am today. I have learned that I have the power to control my own destiny and that by looking at things from different perspectives, I can find true meaning in life.

Nurturing Influence

My parents were wonderful and greatly influenced my beliefs, values, and way of life. Looking back, I realize how much of their personalities, thoughts, actions, and attitudes I adopted.

My father was very curious and always seeking to expand his knowledge. He did this by reading metaphysics books, experimenting, and sharing his learning. I remember one particular experiment where he built a pyramid made of cardboard, which he hung above his and my mother's bed using a pulley system. He wanted to explore the myths surrounding pyramid energy, and his curiosity and desire to experiment were at the core of who he was. He was interested in New Age ideas long before they became popular.

My mother had a deep passion for creativity and always sought to learn and try new things, whether it be in cooking, sewing, gardening, or art. She put great dedication and effort into everything she did and derived joy from it. She taught me to love and strive for growth in my pursuits and to give my all. As a homemaker, she also instilled in me the importance of independence. I particularly remember a conversation with her where she emphasized the feeling of liberation, which encouraged me to learn how to drive a car. Her words stayed with me and I saved up from my part-time job to pay for driving lessons and eventually obtain my driver's license.

My parents instilled in me a strong desire to grow and develop. They never said something was impossible; instead, when they set their minds to something, they took action. Their example taught me to learn from my successes and mistakes and strive to do better in the future.

I learned the value of listening through my father, which made talking to him pleasurable. My mother's fearless spirit taught me to stand up for myself. They also gave me a strong determination to pursue my passions and satisfy my curiosity, which I did as a teenager by becoming a musician and even the first female trombonist in my country. I loved it!

My life changed dramatically in 1997 when I got married, and my mother passed away; in 2001, my father also passed away.

At that time, all the things my parents had instilled in me were pushed to the background as I struggled to cope with my loss.

What are we to do when adversity strikes?

Crumbling World

I did not realize that my ex-husband had systematically cheated and deceived me for years with my family and friends. Shortly after my father's death, my ex absconded, leaving me to face the moneylenders and banks to pay off his accumulated debts.

One of the outstanding events was that on my way home, I received a call from my aunt who lived in an apartment opposite my house. She sounded tense and upset and told me not to go home but to drive straight to her place. The moneylenders had been waiting for me outside my house for some time. I felt petrified and had heavy heart palpitations as I peered out of my aunt's bedroom window and watched them parked in front of my house, waiting for me. And this feeling lasted until the next day when I had to sneak home to prepare for work, by which time they had left.

We had to sell our family home to pay off the debt. My whole family, including my brothers and extended family, were involved in the entire drama to help and support me through the mess I was facing.

My fear was so great that I suppressed emotions to keep that fear at bay. I had become entirely numb, without feeling or a future in sight. I was confused and did not know what to do - fear for my safety and security crept in and caused chaos inside.

All I knew was that I was alone, had no home, was financially ruined and did not know how to start my life over. My anchors were gone, and many feelings of fear, insecurity, helplessness and uncertainty were prevalent. My whole life was spiraling out of control, and I did not know how to navigate this new environment.

Depression quickly set in.

After the fiasco with the moneylender, my brother and family opened their doors for me to stay for a while. One evening, sitting alone in the dark, I was overcome by an overwhelming sense of loneliness, guilt and shame. And a heartbreaking and deep cry erupted from my soul and the pit of my stomach, mixed with despair and anger at everything. At that moment, I felt at my lowest, to the point where I questioned my life and my mortality. Was my life, as it was, worth living? And at that moment, I prayed for my parents to take me with them.

How do we find ourselves when we are disillusioned with reality?

Why Me? Phase Sets in

It is incredible how the defense mechanism kicked in as I went through the stages of denial, devaluation and passive aggression. I was fully engaged in erasing and distorting the world around me. Super-sensitive is an understatement when well-meaning people say, "You are strong", "You'll get over it", and "Do not worry ". And often, I had the natural urge to cry out, "Are you kidding me? How do you know I am strong? I do not want to be strong."

It was difficult to feel better when my energy, hope and drive were drained and exhausted. So, I pushed family and friends away and reinforced my coping mechanism by giving my all to my work and sacrificing long hours. And when I got home exhausted, my only

relaxation was watching Pride and Prejudice, the BBC version. This obsession continued for three years - every day. This created a little bubble where

I felt safe and created a new reality where I was in control while everything else was in chaos.

I did not want to feel what I felt. I did not want to feel sadness, grief, guilt, shame or anything else. All I wanted was to suppress and numb my feelings so I could get through them as painlessly as possible.

I began to isolate myself and push people away. In this state of vulnerability, I kept my circle tight. And in any life-changing situation, as the saying "problems never come alone" shows, there is always a natural decluttering process that is a blessing in disguise.

In one of my childhood best friends, I had a trusted confidant. In many conversations where I poured my heart out to her, I discovered that she betrayed me to my other friends and turned them against me. To give context: This betrayal and hurt felt worse than what my husband did by running away from his responsibilities. Knowing how my words can be interpreted to suit someone else's intentions was a valuable lesson.

Of course, the circle of people I trusted became even narrower at that moment. I discovered the value of trusting my family and friends while the universe helped me declutter my relationships. They were my saving grace by supporting and giving me the space to heal. They came to me in my deepest and darkest moments and helped bring me back into the light.

How do we find ourselves when we are disillusioned with reality?

Grasping for Change

I started to see big changes in myself, but it was hard to accept at first. I liked feeling like a victim and telling my sad story to anyone who would listen.

I clung to feeling like a victim and my suffering, treating it as if it was a part of me. I saw it as my badge of honor. But eventually, I realized I needed to take responsibility for everything that happened to me because it was meant to happen.

I understood that I no longer wanted to identify as a victim or hold onto a negative mindset; it went against everything my parents taught me and what I truly believed in. I was determined to make a change.

I realized that I had lost sight of myself and was questioning my value, self-acceptance, my reasons to live and my goals in life. To manifest the life I desired, I needed to find ways to shift the limiting beliefs that were hindering me.

I set out to heal and grow internally by being curious and making connections. My aim was to uncover the depths of my conscious and subconscious mind.

To make it manageable, I started by rebuilding my sense of self by asking the fundamental question "Who am I?". It would be a difficult journey, but it was a necessary starting point.

How do we rebuild our lives and identities from the ground up when everything falls apart?

Questions as a Compass

On my journey of self-discovery, I faced many questions. I needed to use qualities I had ignored in myself, like courage and strength, to find answers. I had to use all my resources to change and discover things about myself.

I started by looking at my biggest problem with loving and believing in myself. This problem was so strong that it caused many hurtful memories and actions that held me back. I thought I didn't deserve to love or be nice to myself, and I was surprised by how many tears I cried during this discovery process.

I noticed the things I said to myself and how I reacted to different situations. I saw that I didn't treat myself with respect, didn't believe in myself and noticed my thoughts, patterns and habits that weren't helpful.

One important realization was that I wasn't the voice in my head. It was a voice that judged and scared me, making things worse in my mind and how I reacted externally.

I worked hard to understand the beliefs that held me back, and I learned more and found new ways to overcome these obstacles. I read books and learned about meditation and healing practices to reach my full potential.

It was hard to see the truth, but I had to do it. And when it was hard, I knew it was important to keep working. I used my curiosity, resilience and faith as my guide.

"What if I fail?" I used to be scared of this question. But then I understood that failing and making mistakes are chances for me to grow and get better. Instead of being afraid of them, I learned to accept and learn from them. I realized that it's not only about reaching the end but also about enjoying the way there.

Changing my thinking gave me more confidence and helped me be in control of my emotions, energy, thoughts, and beliefs. It helped me see things differently and respond differently.

How can we use our feelings to influence our behavior and create the energy that inspires and motivates us daily?

The Gift of Emotions

For years I allowed others to influence my behavior and reactions by giving them my control.

I remember how a former boss intimidated me so much that I lost my confidence and felt miserable. As the stress became more and more unbearable, I thought of quitting my job. I did a lot of internal work to understand the situation, and early one morning, the glass ceiling above my head shattered.

I realized that everything my boss was saying to me in a derogatory way reflected her own feelings. It was not about me. Her coping mechanism was that she thought she was in control when she was not. I realized that I had made it easy for her to manipulate me by allowing her to control me by getting me to react, even to the smallest reaction.

When that glass ceiling shattered, I realized that people like my ex-boss cause suffering when they suffer. I need to find that compassion for them, only then can I find it for myself. I felt free and empowered when I stopped responding to her toxic taunts. Needless to say, she lost interest soon after.

I used the saying "I take back my remote control" to remind me when I faced similar situations. It helped me understand my feelings and reactions better. I learned that emotions are helpful and can guide me. But I also had to give myself time to think and be honest with myself about why I felt a certain way. It took some time to not be afraid and accept myself, but I had to keep letting go of that fear. With practice, I got better at understanding my emotions and aligning my energy with them.

I changed the way I thought about "negative" emotions and started to see them in a different way. For example, I saw frustration as something that helps me keep going, mistakes as a way to learn, complex challenges as a chance to grow, fear as something that makes me brave, being vulnerable as a sign of strength, and believing in myself as powerful. This helped me feel better about these emotions and know that I would be okay even when I was feeling them.

Amber Rae says in her book The Answer Lies Within You that fearlessness is a myth. "An unnecessary and unattainable goal ... Fear is not your enemy ... Fear has been ingrained in your system for millions of years as a protective mechanism. The truth is that you need your fear. "

Venturing into the World of the Subconscious

My sense of identity and purpose became more apparent as I delved deeper into understanding myself. This helped me see the difference between feeling powerless and having power. Even when others held different viewpoints, I examined my own beliefs critically. This inner examination also allowed me to find peace and quiet, creating space for contemplation. I knew then that I was on the right path.

I sought out other people, particularly those who were also on a journey of self-discovery, and I listened to their ideas and perspectives. Though I enjoyed the freedom of exploring and experimenting, I found that the lack of structure made it hard to maintain consistency in my practice.

As I continued, I gained insights into my challenges and realized that I had many limiting beliefs tucked away in my subconscious. It was like opening

Pandora's box- understanding my patterns and habits led me deeper into the complexities of my subconscious.

Our subconscious often tries to communicate with us, but we are not always listening. Any emotions that cause us discomfort is usually a sign from our subconscious that we need to change our ways of thinking or acting.

So, I set out to reprogram my subconscious to work for me so that I could develop new, powerful habits and ways of thinking. I was looking for solutions that were easy to use and would help me harness my unpleasant emotions- such as fear, frustration, and challenges- to align my beliefs and behaviors with my goals and purposes.

How can we reach our subconscious faster to change our limiting beliefs to our advantage?

Connecting the Dots with NLP

I explored the world of Neuro-Linguistic Programming (NLP) and found that it helped me connect different systems, techniques, and tools to change my perspective and reach my goals. I learned how to reprogram my subconscious mind and install new, empowering beliefs. This helped me reduce the negative thoughts and "dramatic stories" that were holding me back.

I had worked in the aviation industry for over 33 years and have had a successful career. But in my 31st year, I started to feel like something was missing, and I wanted to pursue other goals. I ignored these feelings for two years but eventually realized I needed to change. I used NLP backward planning to clarify my next steps, which gave me the courage to leave my job and follow my heart.

I also found the concept of anchors helpful in connecting with different feelings and states of mind. An example of my favorite anchor is listening to music with meaningful lyrics during my morning walks. It helps me start my day on a positive note and align my emotions with my goals.

NLP also helped me overcome my tendency to be a perfectionist and procrastinator. I learned that taking action, even if it's not perfect, is more important than constantly planning. By doing this, I was able to move forward and make progress.

Have a Care: NLP is not a solution for all problems. It's essential for those who want to change to take responsibility for their own growth and be willing to put in the effort to change.

This process requires being honest with yourself and being willing to work through challenges and discomfort. It's also important to remember that progress is not always linear and that taking things at your own pace is okay. Instead, focus on learning from mistakes and growing from them.

How can we raise awareness to understand better and support each other?

We are All Connected

When I think back on my journey and all the challenges I've faced, I realize that what I went through is not unique. Many people have similar experiences and feelings, like feeling lonely or not feeling good enough. But I also realize that my parents helped shape me into who I am today. They taught me to be persistent, to explore new things and to be creative.

I want to share five important lessons I've learned:

Lesson #1: *What are we to do when adversity strikes?*

Power of Self-Reflection:

Our minds have great power and can accomplish the seemingly impossible if we set them free. However, over time, we often develop distorted perceptions and beliefs that make life seem more complex than it needs to be. This happens when we fall into the habit of accepting these perceptions as truth. To change this, we must take responsibility for our actions and thoughts and actively seek self-reflection.

Through self-reflection and curiosity, we can better understand our thoughts, emotions, and actions and ask ourselves why we feel the way we do. We can also examine our language and look for unresolved issues within ourselves.

By practicing self-compassion and confronting our weaknesses and faults, we can better understand ourselves and what works for us and what doesn't.

Lesson #2: *How do we find ourselves when we are disillusioned with reality?*

Follow Your Heart and Intuition

Change can be scary, but it takes courage to make it happen. We often feel uncertain and insecure, and our natural response is to be afraid. We have learned to ignore our intuition, but the truth is the only thing to be afraid of is not listening to ourselves.

When we speak from the heart, it's the voice of our true selves. This inner voice gives us direction and helps us stay true to who we are, which leads to happiness.

To start, we can take time to listen to our inner voice by breathing and giving it space to speak to us. The most important thing is to stay true to ourselves and keep moving forward, one day at a time.

Lesson #3: How do we rebuild our lives and identities from the ground up when everything falls apart?

Insatiable Curiosity

To navigate a complex world where confusion and inconsistency is common, it is important to be curious and ask questions. Don't be afraid to ask basic questions without worrying about others' opinions. As we find answers, new questions may arise, but through exploring, experimenting and looking for different perspectives, we can gain understanding and growth.

Lesson #4: How can we use our feelings to influence our behavior and create the energy that inspires and motivates us daily?

Art of Letting go of Limiting Beliefs

We often try to control everything, but the more we try to change certain situations and painful memories, the harder it becomes. Our emotional baggage can hold us back, making it difficult to move forward and find answers. Instead of making the world conform to our desires, we should focus on our reactions and feelings. By trusting ourselves, letting go of self-judgment, and accepting and surrendering fear, we can release these blocks and trust the process of letting them go. Remember, the choice and responsibility are ultimately up to us, and we must keep working on it.

Lesson #5: How can we reach our subconscious faster to change our limiting beliefs to our advantage?

Focus on Taking Action

We become so complacent about what we want to do. Take action to make a difference and do what is right. There is no room for excuses, only the responsibility to strive for what you want every day. Reflect on why this change is important to you and take ownership of the results you desire. Remember, where your focus goes, your energy flows and, with it, the power to manifest your desires.

Is it possible to do this? Definitely yes!

With determination in our hearts and a fire in our souls, we can overcome any obstacle that comes our way. We have the power to change our circumstances and shape our own destinies.

We must remember that we are not alone in this journey, for we have the support of a loving community that will stand by us every step.

Remember, it's not the load that breaks us but the way we carry it. As we navigate the twists and turns of life, let us carry our burdens with grace and resilience. Let us learn from our struggles, grow stronger from them, and let them be stepping stones on our path to greatness.

As a coach, I know there are ways to find healing and peace in difficult times. Believe in a better way of life, let go of the expectation for perfection and appreciate and be grateful for the lessons life teaches us.

Stay curious, stay adventurous.

ACKNOWLEDGEMENTS

We would like to express our heartfelt gratitude to everyone who contributed to the making of this book. Writing this book would not have been possible without the support and encouragement of many individuals.

First and foremost, we would like to thank our co-authors who have poured their knowledge and expertise into this book. Your passion and dedication have truly made this book a success.

We would also like to express our gratitude to our families and friends who supported us throughout the process of writing this book. Your love, patience, and understanding have kept us going through the ups and downs of this journey. Your guidance, encouragement, and insightful feedback have helped us shape this book into its final form.

We would like to acknowledge the support of our team, who believed in this project and helped bring it to fruition. Your professionalism, expertise, and commitment to quality have been invaluable.

Finally, we would like to thank our readers for their interest in this book. We hope that the ideas and strategies we have presented will be helpful in improving your lives. Your support and feedback will always be appreciated.

Thank you all for your contributions to this book. It has been a pleasure to work with you and we look forward to future collaborations.

Printed in Poland
by Amazon Fulfillment
Poland Sp. z o.o., Wrocław
06 April 2023

d1f33371-8c45-42d2-b9ef-fc59d783eb68R01